A THREE-FOLD MINISTRY:

IN ACCORDANCE WITH

SCRIPTURE AND CHURCH HISTORY.

BY

The Rev. JAMES R. LESLIE, M.A.,

INCUMBENT OF S. JOHN'S, PORTSOY.

"A three-fold cord is not quickly broken."—*Eccles.* iv. 12.

ABERDEEN: A. BROWN & CO.

EDINBURGH: S. S. ANDERSON. GLASGOW: MENZIES & CO.

MDCCCLXXIII.

Printed by A. King and Co., Letterpress Printers and Stereotypers,

Clark's Court, 2 Upperkirkgate, Aberdeen.

A THREE-FOLD MINISTRY.

MUCH has been said of late regarding Church Government, and many a hazy idea has been promulgated. Perhaps, therefore, a small contribution towards clearing the matter of some of its fogs and mists may not be out of place.

It is always well to have a clear definition, so before proceeding further, we shall settle first of all what is meant by the term Church Government. Two meanings may be attached to it, the one a narrower, the other a wider. In the *wider* sense, it includes discipline, rites, ceremonies, &c., but as it is not our intention to dwell on this meaning, we shall here dismiss it with the remark that in this sense, as Hooker sufficiently proved against the Puritans of his day, the Church may lawfully alter and modify her government from time to time as she shall see fit.

In the *narrower* sense, Church Government refers to the Christian Ministry, which, as we hope to be able to show, is of divine authority, and being so, can be altered only by that divine authority which originally instituted it. It is under this latter head that our subject falls.

The objection has been urged against a three-fold ministry that it is unscriptural and unhistorical. Thus, for instance, in a recent review in one of our leading Northern Journals,* there occurs the following passage :—"We wonder how sensible men can be found who hold the theory of a three-fold ministry. With Scripture and Church History so decidedly against them, there must be some strange infatuation which induces able and good men to cling doggedly to such a theory." But are Scripture and Church History against a three-fold ministry? Nay, so far from being against, they are actually in favour of this form of Church Government. In the following pages we purpose to show the grounds on which we affirm such to be the case.

I.—THE SCRIPTURAL ARGUMENT.

With regard to the Scriptural Argument, it is to be remarked that we are not to expect to find any *systematic*

* The *Banffshire Journal.*

account of the Church in the New Testament. In this respect, there is a striking contrast between the Church of the Old and the Church of the New Dispensation. The children of Israel had not yet entered the Promised Land, their system of Church Polity could not yet be brought into operation, when the Mosaic law was given them. Hence it was needful to be minutely accurate in prescribing that Polity.* But no such necessity lay on the New Testament writers. The Church was already in existence for a considerable number of years before a single book of the New Testament was written,† its machinery was all in operation, and so there was no need for the inspired writers to present their readers with a formal description of that which was daily before their eyes. Mere references to the Church's discipline and polity are then the utmost we can expect. Now, do such references point to a three-fold ministry or not? Assuredly they do. For, as in the Jewish Church there was the three-fold ministry of the High Priest, the Priests, and the Levites, so do we find the exact antitype‡ of this ministry in the New Testament; only as far

---

* "When they further dispute, that if any such thing" (as Episcopal Government) "were needful, Christ would in Scripture have set down particular statutes and laws appointing that Bishops should be made, and prescribing in what order, even as the Law doth for all kind of officers which were needful in the Jewish regiment ; might not a man that would bend his wit to maintain the fury of the Petrobrusian heretics, in pulling down oratories, use the self-same argument with as much countenance of reason ? If it were needful that we should assemble ourselves in Churches, would that God, which taught the Jews so exactly the frame of their sumptuous Temple, leave us no particular instructions in writing, no not so much as which way to lay any one stone ? Surely such kind of argumentation doth not so strengthen the sinews of their cause, as weaken the credit of their judgment, which are led therewith."—*Hooker, Eccles. Polity*, B. VII., § 13.

† The Gospel according to S. Matthew was written first, and its publication cannot by any possibility be placed earlier than eight years after our Lord's Ascension. (*Alford's Greek N. Test.*, Vol. I., *Proleg.* p. 30.) But considering its object we could not expect to find any account of the Christian Ministry in it. Only in the Acts of the Apostles and in the Epistles could we reasonably look for any such account. The first of the Epistles, viz. :—1 Thessalonians was written A.D. 52 (*Alford's Greek N. Test.*, Vol. III., *Proleg.* p. 47), i.e., it fits in at the beginning of Acts xviii. But the Church was in full working order before that time, so much so, that two chapters before we read of a General Council having been held at Jerusalem, A.D. 50.

‡ It is a well known maxim of S. Augustine's, "in veteri Testamento est occultatio novi, in Novo Testamento est Manifestatio veteris" (the

as the substance surpasses the shadow, the thing typified, the type, so far does the Christian ministry surpass the Jewish.

During our Lord's lifetime, there was the three-fold ministry of Himself; the twelve Apostles (S. Mark iii. 13-19), and the seventy disciples (S. Luke x. i.). Before His Ascension, our Lord, who was sent by the Father to be the Chief Shepherd and High Priest of the New dispensation (Heb. iii. 1; 1 Peter ii. 25), and who had Himself received an actual consecration to the glory of the priesthood (Heb. v. 5), commissioned the twelve Apostles to occupy the first rank in the ministry, giving them power to ordain others, and promising to be with them and their successors " unto the end of the world."

This commission was couched in the amplest and most authoritative terms: " As my Father hath sent Me, even so send I you. And when He had said this, He breathed on them, and saith unto them, Receive ye the Holy Ghost: Whose soever sins ye remit, they are remitted unto them ; and whoso soever sins ye retain, they are retained. (S. John xx.

New Testament is enclosed in the Old, the Old is unfolded in the New). And on this principle alone, we should, even before examination, expect an analogy between the Jewish and the Christian ministries.

Such analogy is not fanciful. It is frequently pointed out by the early Fathers of the Church (*e.g.*, by Clemens Romanus, 1 Cor. xl. ; Jerome Ep. 101 to Evang.); but it does not rest merely on their authority. There is *Scriptural* authority for it—Psalm cxxxii. 16; Isaiah lxvi. 21; Jerem. xxxiii. 18, 20, 21; Mal. i. 11; Heb. v. 4. " We may," says Dr. Barrow (speaking of Psalm cxxxii.), " solidly and safely conclude, that this promise" (of perpetuity) " doth principally belong, and shall therefore infallibly be made good, to the Christian Priesthood ; to those who, in the Christian Church, by offering spiritual sacrifices of praise and thanksgiving, by directing and instructing the people in the knowledge of the Evangelical law, by imploring for and pronouncing upon them the Divine benediction, do bear analogy with, and supply the room of, the Jewish Priesthood."

That this analogy must necessarily encroach upon the prerogatives of the *One Mediator* between God and man, we deny. The objection would tell equally against the Jewish ministry.

If it be objected that all Christians are now called Kings and Priests (1 Peter ii. 9; Rev. i. 6, v. 10), and that therefore there can be no separate Order of Priests, it must also be borne in mind that the Jews themselves are called " a kingdom of *priests*, a holy nation" (Exod. xix. 6), and that notwithstanding these appellations, they had a separate Order of priests. It is indeed difficult to see what is the difference between this objection and the " gainsaying of Core," so strongly rebuked by S. Jude (v. 11).

21-23.) "All power is given unto Me in heaven and in earth. Go ye therefore, and teach all nations, baptizing them in the name of the Father, and of the Son, and of the Holy Ghost : Teaching them to observe all things whatsoever I have commanded you : and lo, I am with you alway, even unto the end of the world." (S. Matt. xxviii. 18-20.) *

We now have the twelve, the seventy,† to which two orders was soon afterwards added—the third order of Deacons. (Acts vi. 1-6.) ‡ Again, we hear of the three-fold

* "The regular transmission of ministerial powers and authority from our Lord to the Apostles, from the Apostles to the Bishops whom they ordained, from these Bishops to others, and so on to our own or any other time, is called the Apostolical Succession. It can be traced up by many Churches, including our own, in an unbroken order, the names of a vast number of Bishops having been preserved ; and as each Bishop has always, ordinarily, been ordained by at least three Bishops (and often by more), either of whom would have been sufficient for the purpose, the chains of connection between modern Bishops and the Apostles are very numerous. The Episcopate of the Church of England is in the strictest historic sense an Apostolic Succession, for every Archbishop of Canterbury can be distinctly traced up to S. Augustine in the year 605, or to Theodore, Archbishop of Canterbury, in the year 668. S. Augustine was consecrated by Virgilius, Archbishop of Arles, and Theodore by Vitalian, Bishop of Rome. The latter, at least, can be distinctly shown to have derived his succession from S. Clement, the 'fellow-labourer' of S. Paul, and the first Bishop of Rome after the Apostles themselves ; while it is almost as certain that 'Trophimus the Ephesian' was the first Bishop of Arles. But the habit of ordaining Bishops in the way I have spoken of was so universally established in the Church all over the world, that if there were no historic evidence remaining of this exact character, the highest human certainty would exist that all Bishops up to the time of the Reformation had been ordained by other Bishops in regular succession from the time of our Lord."—*Blunt's Household Theology*, p. 99.

† Seventy—the exact number may have been *seventy-two*, a multiple of twelve (the number of the tribes)—after the number of the heads of the house of Israel, and of the *Elders* appointed by Moses, and of the *Palm-trees* at Elim. S. Augustine, speaking of the seventy-two disciples says, "As no one doubts that the twelve Apostles foreshadowed the Order of Bishops, so also we must know that these seventy-two represented the Presbytery (that is the second order of priests)."—*Catena Aurea*, Vol. IV., Part I., p. 344.

‡ Up to this time there were two Orders of Ministers in the Church— *Apostles* and *Presbyters;* now, under the direction of the Holy Ghost, the Apostles institute a third Order—that of *Deacons.*"
"The institution of this Order arose from an occasion of a secular kind, though not altogether so ; for the Tables were in some respects sacred ; and, as *Bp. Pearson* here observes, the office to which these seven were

appointed was not only œconomical, but ecclesiastical. Men *full* of the *Holy Ghost* and wisdom were chosen (v. 3), and they were ordained with prayer and laying on of hands of the Apostles (v. 6) ; and having been so chosen and ordained, they performed the sacred functions of baptizing and preaching the Word (Acts viii. 36, 38) ; but they are distinguished from the Apostles, in that they could not administer confirmation (viii. 14, 15)."

"On the necessity of the Order of *Deacons*, as well as of Bishops and Presbyters, to the due constitution of a Church, *S. Ignatius* says, Epistle to the Trallians 3, 'let all reverence the Deacons as an appointment of Jesus Christ, and the Bishop as Jesus Christ who is the Son of the Father, and the Presbyters as the Sanhedrim of God and Assembly of the Apostles. Apart from these, there is no Church.'"

"These Seven are not here *called* by the *name* which the Church in the time of the Apostles, and ever since, has assigned to the third Order of Ministers, viz., the name of *Deacons*."

"But this is according to the ordinary manner of the writer of the Acts of the Apostles. We do not hear of the imposition of the word *Ecclesia* [Church] on the society of believers. [Compare also the imposition of the word Christians.] But the Society is formed first, and then a *name* (not a *new word*, but one already in use) is used in speaking of it."

"So it was with all the three Orders in the Church. First the *thing existed ;* there was no display made in giving it a name—but a word is used to describe the thing, already received and practised in the Church. A striking instance of this may be seen in the first mention of Presbyters or Elders, xi. 30, where we find that they have been already installed, and were exercising authority in the Church, before we have ever heard of their name."

"So it is here. Seven men are appointed, and it is said, not without some prophetic intimation of their future name, that their office is διακονεῖν [diaconein] τραπέζαις (to serve tables). The manner of their election and ordination is carefully described ; their functions and acts are recorded. And so the matter rests for a time. But when we come to read the Epistles of S. Paul, we find an Order of the Church in well-defined existence, and with functions fully recognized—and *that* Order is *there* called, by a name then generally known, the Order of *Deacons* (Phil. i. 1 ; 1 Tim. iii. 8, 12), and that Order can be traced downward from those Epistles through the writings of the early Fathers."

"No other time has ever been assigned for the *appointment* of *Deacons*, than the occasion which is described in this chapter and which has been regarded from ancient times as the date of their institution."

"Accordingly the *Church of England*, which declares that 'it is evident unto all men, diligently reading the Holy Scripture, and ancient Authors, that from the Apostles' time there have been these Orders in Christ's Church—*Bishops, Priests, and Deacons*' (Preface to the Ordinal), says, in the heading of this Chapter in the Authorized Version, that 'the Apostles appoint to the office of *deaconship* seven chosen men, of whom Stephen, a man full of faith and of the Holy Ghost, is one;' and in her office for the Ordering of Deacons, she says, that 'God did inspire the Apostles to choose into the Order of *Deacons* the first martyr, S. Stephen, with others ;' and she appoints the beginning of this chapter of the Acts to be read as an Epistle at the Ordering of Deacons."—*Wordsworth on Acts* vi. 3-6, *Greek Test.*, Vol. I., p. 63.

order of, *first*, Apostles, also Angels (Rev. i. 20); * *secondly*
Presbyters, *i.e.*, Elders or Bishops, *i.e.*, Overseers (Acts xi. 30;
xiv. 23; xv. 2, 4, 6, 22, 23; xvi. 4; xx. 17, 28; Phil. i. 1;
1 Tim. iii. 1, 2; v. 17, 19; Titus i. 5, 7; James v. 14;

* In the Apocalypse, "we find our blessed Saviour sending messages or
Epistles by the Apostle John, to the Angels of the Seven Churches
of Asia. Who these Angels were, is a point for careful consideration.
That they were, in our popular sense, Angels, that is heavenly spirits, is
too absurd to be maintained." [For had they been so, S. John would
not have been commanded to *write* to them. "A written revelation is
intended for men, not for heavenly spirits."] "A second supposition
might be, which is equally unreasonable, that the Angels of the Churches
were the Churches themselves; for, in the explanation of S. John's vision,
at the conclusion of his first chapter, the candlesticks, which represent the
Seven Churches, are clearly distinguished from the Seven Stars, which are
emblems of the Angels. Nor, thirdly, would it be a satisfactory
hypothesis to explain the term in question, as meaning a collective body
or Presbytery. These angels are always addressed as individuals, and not
as Colleges. For each of them is always addressed in the singular number.
There is no example, under similar circumstances, throughout the sacred
volume, of the same mode of expression being used towards a collective
body."

"After ascertaining that the Angels in the Apocalypse were individual
persons, our next inquiry is with respect to their rank and jurisdiction in
the Church. That they were important persons, and occupied a high
official station, appears from our Lord's selection of them, before all others,
to receive and communicate His divine messages. Indeed the word
Angel is frequently used in the sacred writings as an appellation necessarily
implying distinction and authority. Among the Jews the High Priest
was often termed Angel, from the idea that he was God's messenger; as
also were the rulers of the Synagogue, who were often termed Angels of the
Congregation. And the Angel of the Congregation had under him
inferior ministers, corresponding to the Presbyters and Deacons of the
Christian Church. In the prophecies of Malachi, our Lord Himself is
termed the Angel of the Covenant. And as the titles Angel and
Apostle are very nearly synonymous—an *Apostle* means a person empowered
to deliver a message, and an *Angel* a person who actually delivers it"
[*i.e.*, the word *Apostle* points more prominently to the *Mission*, the word
Angel to the *Message*]—"we find the Apostles actually called Angels in
the very book now before us." (Rev. xxi. 12, 14.)

"The high preogatives belonging to the Apocalyptic Angels, or as we
should term them, Bishops of the Seven Churches, are remarkably
apparent from the language of our Saviour Himself, addressed to them in
His divine Epistles. He makes them responsible for their respective
Churches. He ascribes to them the powers of jurisdiction and coercion.
He blames some of them for not exerting these powers with sufficient
vigour; He bestows praise on others for their energy and faithfulness.
And it was not merely over the Laity that this spiritual jurisdiction was
exercised; for Presbyters and Deacons undoubtedly existed at that time in
the Asiatic Churches. We read of St. Paul many years before, sending

1 Peter v. 1); * and *thirdly* Deacons (Phil. i. 1; 1 Tim. iii. 8, 10, 12, 13). And it is worthy of observation that there is one verse in Holy Scripture, viz., Phil. i. 1, in which we have all these three orders mentioned together.

The Epistle to the Philippians is addressed to " the Bishops and Deacons," *i.e.*, to the second and third orders. S. Paul and S. Timothy belong to the first order. Why the Epistle is addressed to the second and third orders, and not also to the Bishop of the Philippians (in the modern sense of the word), is, because he had been with S. Paul, and took the Epistle back to Philippi with him. This fact we learn from v. 25 of Chap. ii., where S. Paul says, " I supposed it necessary to send to you Epaphroditus, my brother and companion in labour, and fellow soldier, but your *Apostle* " (for so the word ought to be rendered, and not " messenger," as in the English version). By giving him the name of Apostle, S. Paul plainly shows that the Episcopal office was entrusted to Epaphroditus. †

To the *third* order was entrusted the care of the sick and poor (Acts vi.), and in some instances at least, they were allowed to preach and to baptize (Acts viii. 12, 36-38), ‡ and

from Miletus to Ephesus, ' to call the Presbyters of the Church.' (Acts xx. 17.) To complete this argument, it may be noticed that the very names, in some cases, of these Asiatic Bishops, are still preserved in ancient Church writers. We are, therefore, warranted to affirm (agreeably to the concurring testimony of all ecclesiastical antiquity), that the Angels of the Seven Churches of Asia were Bishops, appointed by the Apostles, and recognised by our blessed Lord Himself, as presiding over Ephesus, Smyrna, Pergamos, Thyatira, Sardis, Philadelphia, and Laodicea."—*Sinclair's Vindication of the Episcopal or Apostolical Succession*, p. 27.

* Presbyter was a name of dignity ; Bishop was a name of office as well as a name of dignity, *i.e.*, descriptive as well as titular. Presbyter and Priest are identical words. Presbyter (the original form) became shortened into Prester, that into Prest, and Prest is now in later times Priest. Apostles are called Elders (*i.e.*, Presbyters) in 1 Peter v. 1 ; 2 John i. ; and 3 John i. But are we therefore to regard the two names as identical ? No ; for *then* all Apostles were Elders, but not every Elder an Apostle ; just as *now*, every Bishop is a Priest, but not every Priest a Bishop.

† *Theodoret, Comment.* on Phil. i. 1.
" Epaphroditus is by all antiquity reckoned the first Bishop of Philippi." —*Wheatly on the Book of Common Prayer*, p. 98.

‡ S. Philip although not here, yet in Acts xxi. 8, is called Philip the Evangelist. But the title of Evangelist was one of work and not of

to assist at the administration of the Lord's Supper (Acts vi. 2); * hence they were possessed not merely of civil functions, but also of ecclesiastical.

To the *Second Order* was committed the ordinary care of the Congregation (Acts xx. 28; 1 Tim. v. 17; Titus i. 9; 1 Peter v. 1, 2), but no Episcopal functions in the modern sense of the words, that is to say, no power of jurisdiction or of ordination. No power of jurisdiction, for they were subject to the first order, who had authority to receive accusations against them, to admonish, and, in cases requiring such a stringent course, to depose them. (1 Tim. v. 1, 19; Titus iii. 10.) Nor do we read anywhere of their having the power to ordain. That passage in which S. Paul exhorts Timothy to neglect not the gift that was in him *with* the laying on of the hands of the Presbytery (1 Tim. iv. 14), might at first sight seem to assign this power to them. But we must remember that S. Paul in another passage (2 Tim. i. 6) reminds Timothy to stir up the gift of God which was in him *by* the putting on of *his* (S. Paul's) hands. We see then that Timothy was really episcopally ordained. The ordination was *with* the Presbytery, but *by* S. Paul. In conformity with this we may compare the usage of the Western Church from early times, we mean the fact that the Presbyters present lay their hands on the head of the person who is being ordained *with the ordaining Bishop*. But although we make this reference, the " Presbytery " here mentioned may have consisted only of members of the first order, for the Apostles were still Presbyters (1 Peter v. 1), though all Presbyters were not Apostles. If Presbyters had possessed the power of ordination, it is not likely that S. Paul would have left Titus in Crete " to ordain elders in every city " (Titus i. 5), seeing that island had been converted to Christianity long before (Acts ii. 11), and so doubtless possessed many Presbyters of its own for carrying on the work of the ministry amongst its inhabitants.

order. We read of no ordination to the office. Just as we at the present day speak of Deacons as Ministers or Clergymen, so Philip the Deacon is spoken of as Philip the Evangelist.

Cyprian, Ep. 72, § 9, says that the Samaritans were " baptized by *Philip the Deacon*, whom the Apostles had sent."

* These tables were partly common and also sacred, for it is probable that the Holy Eucharist was administered at these daily repasts. *See Pearson on this verse.*

The *First Order* was distinguished from the second by the power of ordination (Acts vi. 6; xiv. 23; 1 Tim. v. 22; 2 Tim. i. 6; Titus i. 5), and the power of jurisdiction—a power which we find S. James * exercising at Jerusalem, Epaphroditus at Philippi (Phil. ii. 25), Timothy at Ephesus (1 Tim. i. 3, &c.), and Titus in Crete. (Titus i. 5, 13, &c.) How a title originally applied to the second order came to be applied to this order we learn from Theodoret (born about A.D. 386). He tells us that "the same persons were originally called indiscriminately Bishops and Presbyters, whilst those, who are now called Bishops, were called Apostles. But afterwards the name of *Apostle* was appropriated to such only as were Apostles indeed, and then the name of *Bishop* was given to those who were before called Apostles." (Com. in 1 Tim. iii.) That is to say, those who were ordained only *mediately* by Christ did not think it meet that they should bear the same name as those who were ordained *immediately* † (*i.e.*, without any human intervention) by Him; not that they meant to imply that they did not belong to the first order, only that humility bade them use the less honourable name. Nor is

---

* "During the great forty days after His resurrection, Christ appeared on ten different occasions. It was a time of the deepest interest and importance. Everything that He then did and said had a more than ordinary significance. In reference to two of those occasions, St. Paul informs us (1 Cor. xv. 7) that He was 'seen of James singly, then of all the Apostles.' And St. Luke further mentions, that 'He spake to them of the things concerning the kingdom of God,' *i.e.*, the Christian Church. Why was S. James singled out for this great distinction? Why, again, do we find him introduced in the history of the Acts, again and again, in such a way as to imply some marked pre-eminence even among the Apostles—a pre-eminence which is nowhere expressly notified or accounted for in the sacred text? The time will not suffer me to produce the passages (Acts xii. 17; xv. 13; xxi. 18. See also Gal. i. 19; ii. 9), though they are all interesting—the more interesting from their *incidental character* —and they admit of only one interpretation. Every reader of ecclesiastical history knows what that interpretation is. St. James was appointed (not improbably by our Lord Himself before His ascension, but if not, certainly by the Apostles very soon after) Bishop of Jerusalem, the first Bishop in the Christian Church."—*On Uniformity in Church Government: a Charge by the Bishop of S. Andrew's*, 1863, p. 18.

† This distinction between an Apostle and a Bishop (in the modern sense of the word), viz., that the one is ordained *immediately*, the other *mediately*, by Christ, may not at first sight seem borne out by the cases of S. Matthias and S. Paul. But what were their cases? S. Matthias was elected by *lot*, *i.e.*, immediately by Christ. And Acts xiii. 3, can only be regarded as referring to S. Paul's special mission to the Gentiles. It

such a change of name by any means a rare occurrence in history. Numerous instances * might be cited. To give but one, the word Emperor which is now applied to certain monarchs was at one time given to the commander even of a single regiment of men.

Other ministerial titles besides the above, such as ' Minister,' ' Evangelist,' ' Preacher,' ' Prophet,' ' Teacher,' ' Pastor,' (Rom. xv. 16 ; 1 Cor. xii. 28 ; Eph. iv. 11 ; 1 Tim. ii. 7, &c.), are used in the New Testament. But they are evidently titles of work and not of order, which might belong, although not necessarily so, either to an Apostle, a Presbyter, or a Deacon (Acts xxi. 8 ; 2 Tim. iv. 5, &c.), and some of them even to lay persons (Acts xxi. 9). They include also those spiritual gifts which were peculiar to the Apostolic age, but which form no part whatever of the permanent ministry of the Church. The possessors of those supernatural gifts caused no breach whatever in the fixed order of the Church. Notwithstanding their gifts they were subject to Apostolic authority. (1 Cor. xiv. 37.) For when any controversy in the Church had to be decided, those who had authority to do so were not "the Apostles and the possessors of spiritual gifts," but " the Apostles and Presbyters." (Acts xv.) Nowhere in the New Testament do we read that the possession of those gifts conferred a spiritual charge such as was committed to Presbyters. We may, therefore, pass the titles in question

cannot be regarded as the account of his ordination to the Apostleship, for he was ordained to that office at the very time of his conversion (Acts xxvi. 17), besides, he himself emphatically denies any human intervention in his ordination. " Paul, an Apostle, not of men, neither by man, but by Jesus Christ," &c. (Gal. i. 1.) Thus he too was ordained *immediately* by Christ.

* " There is no more cause for surprise that an overlooker of *pastors* should afterwards be specially called *Episcopus* [a Bishop], when an over-looker of a *flock* had been previously called so, than that Augustus and all his successors in the Roman Empire should be called *Imperatores* [Emperors], when in the age preceding him, and indeed in his own age, all victorious *Generals*, as Lucullus, Pompey, and Mark Antony, had been called *Imperatores* [Emperors] ; or, that a large combination of provinces should be called *Diocesis* [a Diocese] by and after the Emperor Constantine, when, before his time, a single province had been termed so."—*Theophilus Anglicanus*, p. 90.

Bishop Onderdonk in *Episcopacy Tested by Scripture*, p. 12, gives a long list of similar examples, such as 'President,' 'Governor,' 'Minister,' 'Elder,' 'Consul,' &c. &c.

by without further notice, as not affecting the conclusions at which we have already arrived regarding the Christian Ministry. Only to the three orders, mentioned before, do we read of any ordinations in the New Testament.

We have now gathered together and examined the various scattered references in the New Testament to the Christian Ministry. That ministry we have found to be distinctly three-fold. And what is remarkable about it is, that its various orders derived their authority from above, not from below. We do not read of the first members of the Church raising some from among themselves to a higher position than the equality on which all originally stood. On the contrary, the two lower orders derived their power and authority from the first, the members of which derived their still higher power and authority from the Lord Himself. Our Lord chose the Apostles and made them the sole depositaries of His commission, with all the powers which it conferred. They again, in their turn, delegated such of their powers as were capable of transmission, and necessary for the continuance of the Church, to others, either as their coadjutors or successors. And those to whom they so delegated the full powers of the ministry were not the Deacons nor the Presbyters, but (in the later meaning of the word) the Bishops to whom the second and third orders were subject. *

Having proved a three-fold Ministry to be in accordance with Scripture, we now pass on to make good our second position, that it is in accordance with Church History.

II.—THE HISTORICAL ARGUMENT.

This portion of our subject naturally divides itself into three heads. First, the Ante Nicene Period; secondly, the Period

* Presbyterians and other upholders of parity (none of whom were heard of for 1500 years after the foundation of the Christian Church) cannot lay claim to this succession. At best, their ministers can trace their ordination to no higher source than the second order—an order which has no power to ordain. But they are not sure of being able to do even thus much, for several of their founders or first ministers were merely laymen who pretended to ordain to an office which they themselves had never received. Thus, for instance, "Calvin was neither Priest nor Deacon," but "a French layman."—(*Blunt's Household Theology*, pp. 89 and 195.) Again, in Scotland, "Andrew Melville, the father and founder of Scottish Presbyterianism" was "a layman without any ordination."---(*Stephen's History of the Reformation and Church in Scotland*, pp. 72, 206.)

between the Council of Nicæa and the Reformation ; and, thirdly, the Period since the Reformation.

A.—THE ANTE NICENE PERIOD.

What was the form of Church Government during this period? Such is the question which we have to answer. And it is evident we shall be better able to give a correct reply if we go to the fountain-head itself for our facts, and do not take them at second-hand, and as they come to us, through the distorted vision of same modern writer. We therefore propose to give a Catena * of authorities bearing on the Ministry of the Church, culled from the writings of those who lived in Ante Nicene times. The reader will be able to judge for himself from this Catena, whether the Ministry of the Ante Nicene Church was three-fold or not.

1.—CLEMENT, BISHOP OF ROME.

This Apostolic Father is generally supposed to have been the Clement mentioned by St. Paul as his friend and fellow-worker. (Phil. iv. 3.) The following extracts are from his first epistle to the Corinthians, which may be dated about A.D. 97.

"Ye walked," he writes to them, "in the commandments of God, being obedient to those who had the rule over you,† and giving all fitting honour to the Presbyters among you." (1 Cor., chap. i.)

By the words, "those who had the rule over you," we are to understand the Bishops, so that here we have mention made of the first and second orders in the Ministry, and in the following passage in which the second order is, according to the

---

* In the following Catena the translation is that of Clark's Ante Nicene Library, except in the case of Origen, of whose writings only a part is included in Mr. Clark's series. The dates and particulars about the writers are from the same source. As the editors are Presbyterians, the translation cannot be accused of an Episcopal bias.

† Gr. ἡγούμενοι, Lat. præpositi, i.e., Bishops. The word here evidently points to an intermediate stage between the application of the term Apostle and the term Bishop to the first order. Cyprian speaks of "the chief rulers" [præpositi] "who, by vicarious ordination succeed to the Apostles." —Ep. 68.

New Testament use of the word, still spoken of as "Bishops," we have mention made of the third :—

"The Apostles have preached the Gospel to us from the Lord Jesus Christ; Jesus Christ [has done so] from God. Christ therefore was sent forth by God, and the Apostles by Christ. Both these appointments, then, were made in an orderly way, according to the will of God. Having therefore received their orders, and being fully assured by the resurrection of our Lord Jesus Christ, and established in the word of God, with full assurance of the Holy Ghost, they went forth proclaiming that the kingdom of God was at hand. And thus preaching through countries and cities, they appointed the first fruits [of their labours], having first proved them by the Spirit, to be Bishops and Deacons of those who should afterwards believe." (1 Cor. chap. xlii.)*

And not only does Clement mention the three orders of the Ministry, but he also draws an analogy between the Jewish and the Christian Ministry.

"His own peculiar services are assigned to the High Priest, and their own proper place is prescribed to the Priests, and their own special ministrations devolve on the Levites. The layman is bound by the laws that pertain to laymen. Let every one of you, brethren, give thanks to God in his own order, living in all good conscience, with becoming gravity, and not going beyond the rule of the Ministry prescribed to him." (Chaps. xl. and xli.)†

After recounting how "Moses of old stilled the contention which arose concerning the priestly dignity," Clement proceeds to narrate "the ordinances of the Apostles, that there

---

* We have in this passage the three orders mentioned in the New Testament, viz., 1st, Apostles ; 2nd, Bishops ; and 3rd, Deacons.

† "This, be it observed, is exactly the language of later fathers. In allusion to this resemblance the Presbyters are constantly called *Sacredotes* [Priests] ; the Bishop *Summus Sacerdos* [the High Priest] ; the Deacons, *Levitæ* [Levites]. And it will facilitate our understanding of the whole question if we bear in mind that, as the High Priest was still a Priest, and only distinguished from the other Priests by one or two points of official pre-eminence, so the fathers constantly speak of the Bishop as still a Presbyter (1 Pet. v. 1), but as distinguished from the other Presbyters by the power of ordination and jurisdiction."—*Browne's Exposition of the Thirty-nine Articles*, p. 549.

might be no contention respecting the priestly office." * His words are :—

"Our Apostles also knew through our Lord Jesus Christ, that there would be strife on account of the office of the Episcopate. For this reason, therefore, inasmuch as they had obtained a perfect foreknowledge of this, they appointed those [ministers] already mentioned, and afterwards gave instructions that when these should fall asleep, other approved men should succeed them in their Ministry." (Chap. xliv.)

2.—IGNATIUS.

Ignatius, also an Apostolic Father, was Bishop of Antioch. When Trajan was on his *first* expedition against the Parthians and Armenians, Ignatius voluntarily presented himself before that prince at Antioch, the seat of his Bishopric, and on professing himself a Christian, was condemned to be torn to death by wild beasts at Rome, On his way thither, where he suffered martyrdom on the 20th December, A.D. 107, or according to others, A.D. 116, he wrote epistles to the Ephesians, Magnesians, Trallians, Romans, Philadelphians, Smyrnæans, and to Polycarp. In each of these epistles mention is made, if not of all, at least of one or other of the three orders of the Ministry. We also learn from them the names of various Presbyters and Deacons, and that Onesimus was Bishop of the Ephesians, Damas of the Magnesians, Polybius of the Trallians, and Polycarp of the Smyrnæans. †

a.—To the *Ephesians* Ignatius writes:—"Jesus Christ, our inseparable life, is the [manifested] will of the Father ; as also *Bishops, settled everywhere to the utmost bounds [of the earth],* are so by the will of Jesus Christ." (Chap. iii.) "Wherefore it is fitting that ye should run together in accordance with the will of your Bishop, which thing also ye do. For your justly renowned Presbytery, worthy of God, is fitted as exactly to the Bishop as the strings are to the harp." (Chap. iv.)

* Titles of Chaps. xliii. and xliv., as given in Clark's Ante Nicene Library.

† In proof of Theodoret's statement (quoted p. 16), that after the death of the Apostles the name Bishop was restricted to the first order, we may here observe that Pearson has demonstrated *(Vindic. Ignat.,* Part ii., Chap. 13) that no writer of the second century uses the words Bishop and Presbyter interchangeably. Henceforth the name Bishop is applied to the first order, never to the second. In the case of the extracts given, the reader will be able to verify this for himself.

This epistle, then, bears important testimony to the claims of Episcopacy. For the words which we have italicized show that, in the time of Ignatius, government by Bishops was not a merely local affair, but was the practice of the universal Church.

b.—To the *Magnesians* Ignatius writes:—"I have had the privilege of seeing you, through Damas, your most worthy Bishop, and through your worthy Presbyters, Bassus and Apollonius, and through my fellow-servant, the Deacon Sotio, whose friendship may I ever enjoy, inasmuch as he is subject to the Bishop as to the grace of God, and to the Presbytery as to the law of Jesus Christ." (Chap. ii.)

c.—To the *Trallians* he says:—"Let all reverence the Deacons as an appointment of Jesus Christ, and the Bishop as Jesus Christ, who is the Son of the Father, and the Presbyters as the Sanhedrim of God, and assembly of the Apostles. Apart from these there is no Church." (Chap. iii.) " He who does anything apart from the Bishop, and Presbytery, and Deacons, such a man is not pure in his conscience." (Chap. vii.)

d.—Writing to the *Romans*, he says :—" Sing praise to the Father, through Christ Jesus, that God has deemed me, the Bishop of Syria, worthy to be sent for from the east unto the west." (Chap. ii.)

e.—The *Philadelphians* he exhorts to " give heed to the Bishop, and to the Presbytery, and Deacons." (Chap. vii.) He also bids them " elect a Deacon " as their ambassador, to carry their congratulations to the Church at Antioch on the close of the persecution. " If ye are willing," he says, " it is not beyond your power to do this, for the sake of God, as also the nearest Churches have sent in some cases Bishops, and in others Presbyters and Deacons." (Chap. x.)

f.— To the *Smyrnœans* he writes:—" See that ye all follow the Bishop, even as Jesus Christ does the Father, and the Presbytery as ye would the Apostles ; and reverence the Deacons as being the institution of God. Let no man do anything connected with the Church without the Bishop. Let that be deemed a proper Eucharist, which is [administered] either by the Bishop, or by one to whom he has entrusted it. Wherever the Bishop shall appear, there let the multitude [of the people] also be ; even as, wherever Jesus Christ is, there is the Catholic Church. It is not lawful, without the Bishop, either to baptize or celebrate a love-feast; but whatsoever he shall approve of, that is also pleasing to God, so that everything that is done may be secure and valid." (Chap. viii.)

g.—In his letter to " *Polycarp*, Bishop of the Church of the Smyrnæans," Ignatius says :—" It becomes both men and women who marry, to form their union with the approval of the Bishop, that their marriage may be according to God." (Chap. v.)

The above are only a few out of the many passages which might be cited from the seven shorter epistles of Ignatius, in favour of a threefold ministry. These epistles Pearson (*Vindic. Ignat.*) has fully proved genuine. But if any one prefers the Syriac Version to the Greek, even there does the advocate of a threefold ministry find sufficient evidence for his purpose. Thus, in the epistle to Polycarp, there occurs the following passage :—

" Look ye to the Bishop, that God also may look upon you. I will be instead of the souls of those who are subject to the Bishop, and the Presbyters, and the Deacons; with them may I have a portion in the presence of God." (Chap vi.)

3.—THE MARTYRDOM OF IGNATIUS.

In the " Martyrdom of Ignatius," written by those who accompanied him to Rome, we are told that he visited on his way " the holy Polycarp [formerly] his fellow-disciple, and [now] Bishop of Smyrna. For they had both, in old times, been disciples of St. John the Apostle." Also, that " the cities and Churches of Asia had welcomed the holy man through their Bishops, and Presbyters, and Deacons." (Chap. iii.)

4.—POLYCARP.

Polycarp, " the renowned Bishop of Smyrna," is another of the Apostolic Fathers. His disciple Irenæus tells us that he " was instructed by the Apostles, and was brought into contact with many who had seen Christ." He wrote an epistle to the Philippians which begins in these words : " Polycarp and the Presbyters with him, to the Church of God sojourning at Philippi." We have already seen (p.   ) that Polycarp was called by Ignatius—whose letters, he tells the Philippians in the end of his epistle (Chap. xiii.), he transmits to them at their request—"the Bishop of Smyrna." So that, in this Introduction we have mention made of the first and second orders in the Ministry. And, in the following passage, mention is made of the third order, the Deacons :—" It is needful to abstain from all these things, being subject to the Presbyters and Deacons, as unto God and Christ." (Chap. v.)

5.—HERMAS.

The Pastor of Hermas, the " Primitive Christian's Pilgrim's Progress," was written at a very early period. Although commonly placed amongst the writings of the Apostolic Fathers, yet it was probably published in the reign of Hadrian or of Antoninus Pius. (A.D. 117—A.D. 161.)

In his allegory of the constitution of the Church, Hermas says :—" Hear now with regard to the stones which are in the building. Those square white stones which fitted exactly into each other are Apostles, Bishops, Teachers, and Deacons, who have lived in godly purity, and have acted as Bishops, and Teachers, and Deacons, chastely and reverently to the elect of God." (*Vision Third*, chap. v.)

Pearson (*Vindic. Ignat.*, Part II., Chap. xiii.) by a comparison of passages from the early Fathers in which the word occurs, has shown that the term Teacher is here used by Hermas as equivalent to Presbyter. Hence in the passage cited, three distinct classes of Church officers are enumerated.

6.—HEGESIPPUS.

Hegesippus, the first ecclesiastical historian, flourished in the time of Antoninus Pius and Marcus Aurelius, that is to say, in the middle of the second century. He gives an account of a journey he made to Rome. In it he says :—" The Church of the Corinthians continued in the orthodox faith up to the time when Primus was Bishop of Corinth. . . . On my arrival at Rome, I drew up a list of the succession [of Bishops] down to Anicetus, whose Deacon was Eleutherus. To Anicetus succeeded Soter, and after him [came] Eleutherus." (*Euseb.*, H. E., iv. 22.)

Hegesippus also tells us (*ibidem*) that after the Martyrdom of James the Just, Simeon the son of Cleophas, our Lord's uncle, was unanimously appointed Bishop of Jerusalem; which see continued free from any heresy, till one Thebuthis, disappointed that he was not elected Bishop, began to corrupt it.

This writer, then, mentions the *first* and the *third* orders by name. But although he does not happen to mention the second order, yet, in the three great cities of Jerusalem, Rome, and Corinth, there must have been several Presbyters in each.

7.—LETTER OF THE CHURCHES OF VIENNA AND LUGDUNUM.

In the letter of the Churches of Vienna and Lugdunum to the Churches of Asia and Phrygia, written shortly after A.D. 177, mention is made of "Sanctus, a Deacon from Vienna," and of "Pothinus, who had been entrusted with the service of the Bishopric in Lugdunum." (*Euseb.*, H. E., Book V., chap. i.)

Here we have the *first* and *third* orders enumerated, and in the letter from the same Churches to Eleutherus, Bishop of Rome, we hear of the *second*, when they recommend Irenæus, who was not yet raised to the Episcopate, *among the first as a Presbyter of the Church, the station that he holds*. (*Euseb.*, H. E., Book V., chap. iv.)

8.—IRENÆUS.

Irenæus was born between A.D. 120 and A.D. 140, and lived to A.D. 202. He was the disciple of Papias and Polycarp, both of whom were disciples of S. John, and was first Presbyter, and afterwards Bishop of the Church of Lyons. (*Euseb.*, H. E., Book V., chap. iv.) He not only states that Bishops actually existed in his time, but that they had existed from the beginning, and were successors to the Apostles.

"We are in a position to reckon up," he says, "those who were by the Apostles instituted Bishops in the Churches, and [to demonstrate] the successions of these men to our own times. . . . If the Apostles had known hidden mysteries, which they were in the habit of imparting to the perfect, apart and privily from the rest, they would have delivered them especially to those to whom they were also committing the Churches. For they were desirous that these men should be very perfect and blameless in all things, whom also they were leaving behind as their successors, delivering up their own place of government to these men. . . . Since, however it would be very tedious to reckon up the successions of all the Churches," [he proceeds to reckon up that of the] "Church founded and organized at Rome by the two most glorious Apostles, Peter and Paul," [and to point out] "the faith preached to men, which comes down to our time by means of the succession of the Bishops. . . . The blessed Apostles, then, having founded and built up the Church, committed into the hands of Linus the office of the Episcopate. Of this Linus, Paul makes mention in the Epistles to Timothy. To him succeeded Anacletus; and after him, in the third place from the Apostles, Clement was allotted the Bishopric. . . . To this Clement there succeeded Evaristus. Alexander followed Evaristus; then, sixth from the Apostles, Sixtus was appointed; after him, Telesphorus, who was gloriously martyred; then, Hyginus; after him, Pius; then, after him, Anicetus. Soter having succeeded Anicetus, Eleutherius does now, in the twelfth place from the Apostles, hold the inheritance of the Episcopate. In this order, and by this succession, the ecclesiastical tradition from the Apostles, and the preaching of the truth have come down to us." Irenæus then proceeds to tell us that "Polycarp also was not only instructed by Apostles, and conversed with many who had seen Christ, but was also, by Apostles in Asia, appointed Bishop of the Church in Smyrna." (*Irenæus against Heresies*, Book III., Chap. iii.)

Now, this list is evidently a succession of men in office, and not simply of "eminent leaders." *

In another place Irenæus writes:—"True knowledge is [that which consists in] the doctrine of the Apostles, and the ancient constitution of the Church throughout all the world, and the distinctive manifestation of the body of Christ according to the succession of the Bishops, by which they have handed down that Church which exists in every place, and has come even unto us." (*Against Heresies*, Book IV., Chap. xxxiii.)

Speaking of heretics, he says, "all these are of much later date than the Bishops to whom the Apostles committed the Churches," but "those belonging to the Church are conversant with the same commandments, *and preserve the same form of ecclesiastical constitution*." (*Against Heresies*, Book V., Chap. xx.)

* "Here it is evident that the regular ordination and succession of doctrine in the Church is maintained, not by parity of Presbyters, but by successive ordination of chief Pastors, who in their turn had power to ordain others."—*Browne's Exposition of the XXXIX. Articles*, p. 550.

Irenæus occasionally uses the word Presbyter as a title of age and not of office. Thus, for instance :—" But, again, when we refer them to that tradition which originates from the Apostles [and] which is preserved by means of the successions of Presbyters in the Churches, they object to tradition, saying that they themselves are wiser not merely than the Presbyters, but even than the Apostles, because they have discovered the unadulterated truth." (*Against Heresies*, Book III., Chap. ii.)

This use of the word Presbyter, with reference to age and not to office, is by no means peculiar to Irenæus. It occurs in the writings of Papias and others. Yet it is to be remarked that the writers of the second century never apply the title Presbyter to a Bishop of their own time, but always appropriate it to the second order, to express the distinction between that order and the first. (*Pearson, Vindic. Ignat.*, Part II., Chap. xiii., p. 550.) Whilst doing this, however, they do not scruple to apply the appellation of Presbyters to Bishops of former times, when they wish to call attention not so much to their office, as to their antiquity in the Church. When thus used, the term is equivalent to that of ancients, and might be applied not to one order only, but to all the orders of the ministry. In this sense of "ancients" Irenæus applies it to Polycarp (*Euseb.* H. E., Book V., Chap. 20), and also to certain of the Bishops of Rome. (*Euseb.* H. E., Book V., Chap. xxiv.) But we have already heard him speak of these very persons as if they had sole supremacy in the Church—a supremacy not conferred from below, but derived through succession from the Apostles.

9.—HIPPOLYTUS.

Hippolytus, Bishop of Portus, near Rome, was born soon after A.D. 150, and lived to between A.D. 235 and A.D. 239. " He was a disciple of St. Irenæus, St. Irenæus of St. Polycarp, St. Polycarp of St. John." He speaks of Victor as Bishop of Rome. (*Refutation of all Heresies*, Book IX., Chap. vii.) He tells us that Callistus "propounded the opinion, that if a Bishop was guilty of any sin, . . he ought not to be deposed." About the time of this man, Bishops, Priests, and Deacons, who had been twice married and thrice married, began [to be allowed] to retain their place among the clergy. (*Ibid.*)

10.—CLEMENT OF ALEXANDRIA.

Clement of Alexandria flourished during the latter part of the second and first part of the third centuries. His death took place A.D. 220.

He writes:—"According to my opinion, the grades here in the Church, of Bishops, Presbyters, Deacons, are imitations of the angelic glory. . . . For these taken up in the clouds, the Apostle writes, will first minister [as Deacons], then be classed in the Presbyterate, by promotion in glory (for glory differs from glory) till they grow into a perfect man." *(The Miscellanies,* Book VI., Chap. xiii.)

Again, "Innumerable commands such as these are written in the Holy Bible appertaining to chosen persons, some to Presbyters, some to Bishops, some to Deacons." *(The Instructor,* Book III., Chap. xii.)

11.—TERTULLIAN.

Tertullian, " the earliest Latin Father," flourished from between A.D. 145 or 150 to about A.D. 220.

In his treatise " on Flight in the time of Persecution," Tertullian puts the question :—" When persons in authority themselves—I mean the very Deacons, and Presbyters, and Bishops—take to flight, how will a layman be able to see with what view it is said, " Flee from city to city ? " *(De fuga in Persecutione,* § 11.)

Writing on Baptism, he says, " it remains to put you in mind also of the due observance of giving and receiving baptism. Of giving it, the chief priest (who is the Bishop) has the right : in the next place, the Presbyters and Deacons, yet not without the Bishop's authority, on account of the honour of the Church, which being preserved, peace is preserved." *(On Baptism,* Chap. xvii.)

He challenges heretics to " unfold the roll of their Bishops, running down in due succession from the beginning in such a manner that their first distinguished Bishop shall be able to show for his ordainer and predecessor some one of the Apostles or of Apostolic men—a man, moreover, who continued stedfast with the Apostles. For this is the manner in which the Apostolic Churches transmit their registers ; as the Church of Smyrna, which records that Polycarp was placed there by John ; as also the Church of Rome, which makes Clement to have been ordained in like manner by Peter. In exactly the same way the other Churches likewise exhibit [their several worthies] whom, as having been appointed to their episcopal places by Apostles, they regard as transmitters of the Apostolic seed." (*On Prescription against Heretics*, Chap. xxxi.)

12.—THE APOSTOLICAL CONSTITUTIONS.

Earlier writers were inclined to assign the Apostolical Constitutions to the Apostolic age, and to Clement; but Bunsen thinks that, if we expunge a few interpolations of the fourth and fifth centuries, " we find ourselves unmistakeably in the midst of the life of the Church of the second and third centuries."

In the Apostolical Constitutions, an analogy is drawn between the Jewish and the Christian ministries. "Hear, O thou Holy Catholic Church, . . . these [viz., Bishops] are your High Priests, as the Presbyters are your Priests, and your present Deacons instead of your Levites." (Book II., § 25). "The Bishop, he is the Minister of the Word, the keeper of knowledge, the mediator between God and you in the several parts of your divine worship. . . . He is your ruler and governor; he is your king and potentate; he is next after God, your earthly God, who has a right to be honoured by you." (Book II., § 26.) "If any one does anything without the Bishop, he does it to no purpose." (Book II., § 27.)

The following are the instructions to the Bishop on assembling in Church :—"When thou" [O Bishop] "callest an assembly of the Church, as one that is the commander of a great ship, appoint the assemblies to be made with all possible skill, charging the Deacons as mariners to prepare places for the brethren as for passengers, with all due care and decency. And first, let the building be long, with its head to the east, with its vestries on both sides at the east end, and so it will be like a ship. In the middle let the Bishop's throne be placed, and on each side of him let the Presbytery sit down; and let the Deacons stand near at hand, in close and small girt garments, for they are like the mariners and managers of the ship ; with regard to these, let the laity sit on the other side, with all quietness and good order." (Book II., § 57.)

In the following passage the power of ordination is

assigned to the Bishop alone, and while Presbyters and Deacons are specially mentioned, their duties as of lower grades are also prescribed:—"We command that a Bishop be ordained by three Bishops, or at least by two; but it is not lawful that he be set over you by one; for the testimony of two or three witnesses is more firm and secure. But a Presbyter and a Deacon are to be ordained by one Bishop and the rest of the clergy. Nor must either a Presbyter or a Deacon ordain from the laity into the clergy; but the Presbyter is only to teach, to offer, to baptize, to bless the people, and the Deacon is to minister to the Bishop, and to the Presbyters, that is, to do the office of a ministering Deacon, but not to meddle with the other offices." (Book III., § 20.)

At the end of the eighth book of the Constitutions is a collection of Canons, called *the Apostolical Canons*. Some of them belong to the Apostolic age; others are of a comparatively late date. The first fifty being quoted by the Council of Nicæa, may be regarded as belonging to the period which we are now considering. These fifty "use the word Bishop thirty-six times, in appropriation to him that is the Ruler or President of the Church, above the clergy and laity; twenty-four times the Bishop is expressly distinguished from the Presbyter; and fourteen times indicated as having particular care for government, jurisdiction, censures, and ordinations committed to him." *

The first Canon is, "Let a Bishop be ordained by two or three Bishops." The second, "A Presbyter by one Bishop, as also a Deacon and the rest of the Clergy." The thirty-sixth forbids Bishops to ordain out of their own dioceses. The thirty-eighth decrees that "a Synod of Bishops be held twice in the year." The fortieth forbids "Presbyters and Deacons to do anything without the consent of the Bishop."

13.—ALEXANDER, BISHOP OF JERUSALEM.

"Alexander was at first Bishop of a Church in Cappadocia, but on his visiting Jerusalem he was appointed to the Bishopric of the Church there, while the previous Bishop Narcissus was alive, in consequence of a vision which was believed to be divine. During the Decian persecution he was thrown into prison at Cæsarea, and died there, A.D. 251."

* *Bishop Browne's Exposition of the Thirty-nine Articles*, p. 551.

In "an epistle to the people of Antioch," Alexander mentions two orders of the ministry :—"I have learned that in the providence of God, Asclepiades—who, in regard to the right faith, is most eminently qualified for the office—has undertaken the Episcopate of your Holy Church at Antioch. And this epistle my brethren and masters, I have sent by the hand of the blessed Presbyter Clement." (*Euseb.*, H. E., Book VI., Chap. 11 ; *A. N. L.*, Vol. IX., p. 275.)

14.—ORIGEN.

Origen flourished from about A.D. 185 to A.D. 254. He was a pupil of Clement of Alexandria. He continually mentions the three orders, and distinguishes between them. Bishop Pearson has quoted ten passages from his writings, in seven of which the distinction is plainly marked, in point of order and degree, between Bishops, Presbyters, and Deacons. (*Vindic. Ignat.*, Part I., Chap. 11.) Let the following two suffice as examples of the rest.

In a homily on Ezekiel, speaking of the different penalties which different ranks of offenders incur for the same offence, Origen says :—"Every one shall be punished according to his rank ; if the supreme Governor of the Church offends, he shall receive the greater punishment ; a Layman will deserve lenity in comparison of a Deacon ; a Deacon in comparison of of a Presbyter." (*Hom. V. in Ezek.*)

The antiquity and dignity of a three-fold ministry are referred to by Origen in the following passage :—"There is need of zeal to put down their arrogance who pride themselves on having been brought up Christians by their parents, and especially if they happen to be able to boast of their fathers and forefathers who have been honoured with precedence in the Church, with the throne of a Bishop, or the dignity of the Priesthood, or with the office of Deacon towards God's people." (*Tom. XV.*, 25, 26.)

15.—CYPRIAN.

Cyprian was born about A.D. 200. He was converted to Christ, A.D. 246 by the Carthaginian Presbyter Cæcilius. The year after his baptism he was ordained Deacon ; shortly after Priest ; and in A.D. 248, Bishop of Carthage, which office he held until his martyrdom, A.D. 258.

Numerous were the Epistles which Cyprian, in his enforced retirement from Carthage, addressed as their Bishop to his "Presbyters and Deacons, his beloved brethren." (*Epistles* IV., V., VII., IX., &c.)

Of an insubordinate *Deacon,* Cyprian thus writes:—"Deacons ought to remember that the Lord chose Apostles, that is Bishops and Overseers; while Apostles appointed for themselves Deacons after the ascent of the Lord into heaven, as ministers of their episcopacy and of the Church. But if we may dare anything against God who makes Bishops, Deacons may also dare against us by whom they are made; and therefore it behoves the Deacon of whom you write to repent of his audacity, and to acknowledge the honour of the Priest, and to satisfy the Bishop set over him with full humility." (*Ep.* LXIV. § 3.)

Speaking of certain *Presbyters* guilty of a breach of discipline, Cyprian says:—"What danger ought we not to fear from the Lord's displeasure, when some of the Presbyters, remembering neither the gospel nor their own place, and, moreover, considering neither the Lord's future judgment nor the Bishop now placed over them, claim to themselves entire authority (a thing which was never in any wise done under our predecessors), with discredit and contempt of the Bishop"? (*Ep.* IX., § 1.)

Bishops, Cyprian says, are the "chief rulers, who by vicarious ordination succeed to the Apostles." . . . . "You ought to know that the Bishop is in the Church, and the Church in the Bishop; and if any one be not with the Bishop, that he is not in the Church." (*Ep.* LXVIII., § 4 and § 8.)

Again, Cyprian writes about Bishops:—"Thence, through the changes of times and successions, the ordering of Bishops, and the plan of the Church flows onward; so that the Church is founded upon the Bishops, and every act of the Church is controlled by these same rulers. Since this, then, is founded on the divine law, I marvel that some, with daring temerity have chosen to write to me, as if they wrote in the name of the Church; when the Church is established in the Bishop and the Clergy, and all who stand [fast in the faith]. (*Ep.* XXVI.)

Quotations from this Father might be multiplied to almost any extent, but space forbids us doing more than merely referring to one other passage—his famous passage on the

Episcopate. "The Episcopate is *one*, each part of which is held by each one for the whole." (*On the Unity of the Church*, § 5.) The meaning of this is, that every Bishop's diocese was the whole Church, although for reasons of convenience his jurisdiction was confined to a particular portion of it. (*See Robertson's History of the Church*, Vol. I., p. 163 u.)

16.—DIONYSIUS OF ALEXANDRIA.

Dionysius coming under the influence of Origen, embraced Christianity at an early period of his life. "He was made a Presbyter in Alexandria after this decision; and on the elevation of Heraclas to the Bishopric of that city, Dionysius suceeded him in the presidency of the Catechetical School there, about A.D. 232. After holding that position for some fifteen years Heraclas died, and Dionysius was again chosen to be his successor and ascending the episcopal throne of Alexandria about A.D. 247 or 248, he retained that see till his death, in the year 265." (*A. N. L.*, Vol. XX., p. 157.)

In his epistle to Domitius and Didymus (§ 3), Dionysius says, "I refer to the Presbyters Maximus, Dioscorus, Demetrius, and Lucius. . . . I specify also the Deacons who survived those who died in the sickness." (*Euseb.*, H. E., Book VII., Chap. 11; *A. N. L.*, Vol. XX., p. 203.)

In his epistle to Fabius, Bishop of Antioch, he makes mention of a "certain very aged person of the name of Chœremon, Bishop of the place called the city of the Nile." (*Euseb.*, H. E., Book VI., Chap. 42; *A. N. L.*, Vol. XX., p. 212.)

17.—ARCHELAUS.

Archelaus, Bishop of Cascar, in Mesopotamia, had a memorable disputation with the heretic Manes, in the end of 277 A.D., or the beginning of 278 A.D. In this "Disputation" we are told (§ 39) of one Turbo being ordained a Deacon by Archelaus. We are also told of "a Presbyter whose name was Diodorus," sending to Archelaus a letter couched in the following terms :—"Diodorus sends greeting to Bishop Archelaus." (§ 39.) To this letter Archelaus replied (§ 41) in the following terms :—"Archelaus sends greeting to the Presbyter Diodorus, his honourable son." (*A. N. L.*, Vol. XX., pp. 362, 367.)

18.—The Epistle of the Synod held at Antioch.

A Synod was held at Antioch about A.D. 269, to deal with the case of Paul of Samosata. By this Synod he was convicted, "and a Synodical Epistle was sent on the subject to Dionysius, Bishop of Rome, and to Maximus of Alexandria, and to all the provinces." The Epistle begins thus :—"To Dionysius and Maximus, and to all our fellows in the ministry throughout the world, both Bishops, and Presbyters, and Deacons, and to the whole Catholic Church under heaven, Helenus and Hymenæus, . . . and Lucius, and all the others who are with us, dwelling in the neighbouring cities and nations, both Bishops, and Presbyters, and Deacons, together with the Churches of God, send greeting to our brethren beloved in the Lord." (*Euseb.*, H. E., Book VII., Chap. 30 ; *A. N. L.*, Vol. XIV., p. 402.)

19.—Phileas.

Phileas [A.D. *—307] was Bishop of Thmuis, a town of Lower Egypt. He wrote a letter "in name of other three Bishops, as well as of himself, to Meletius, the Bishop of Lycopolis, and founder of the Meletian Schism." In it he declares that "it is not lawful for any Bishop to celebrate ordinations in other parishes * than his own." (*A. N. L.*, Vol. XIV., p. 444.)

20.—Peter of Alexandria.

Peter [A.D. *—311], Bishop of Alexandria, refers to the above letter, whilst writing to warn his people against Meletius. "I have found out," he says, that Meletius, not "contented with the letter of the most holy Bishops and martyrs," but, "invading my parish, hath assumed so much to himself as to endeavour to separate from my authority the Priests, and those who had been entrusted with visiting the needy." (*A. N. L.*, Vol. XIV., p. 323.)

21.—Alexander, Bishop of Alexandria.

There is also a letter from Alexander (who was Bishop of Alexandria at the time when the Arian controversy arose), to

---

* The word Parish originally meant what we *now* term a Diocese.— *Theophilus Anglicanus*, p 108.

the Catholic Church, intimating the deposition of Arius. To this letter are appended separate lists of Presbyters and Deacons who concurred. (*A. N. L.*, Vol. XIV., p. 353.)

Such is the testimony of an age of persecution, when Bishops, as the heads of the Church, were the especial marks of torture and of death. Surely it is not credible that any would have permitted themselves to be elected to a post of such danger, if they had not believed in the divine origin of Episcopacy. But it is not for their opinions, although these as a rule are certainly worthy of the highest consideration, both on account of the character of the men, and of their nearness to the fountain-head, where the stream is ever the purest,—it is not for their *opinions*, but for their testimony to a matter of *fact*, that we have appealed to the foregoing writers. We have questioned them, not as to what they *thought* was the proper and original form of Church Government, but as to what actually *was* the form which existed in their own days. The answer has been everywhere and uniformly the same. The ministry of the Ante Nicene Church was a threefold ministry. It consisted of the three orders of first Bishops, secondly Presbyters, and thirdly Deacons—the same three orders (although there is a slight change in the names) which we found in the New Testament. Bnt, although the *names* are somewhat changed, there is no change in the *functions*. For, to the first order belonged the power of ordination and of jurisdiction. A Presbyter could, in subordination to his Bishop, teach, celebrate the Eucharist, baptize, bless the people, and perform other such holy offices. A Deacon might occasionally baptize and preach ; and it was his duty to take care of the poor's money, to visit all who stood in need of visitation, and generally to minister to the Bishop and the Presbyters. But neither a Presbyter nor a Deacon could ordain : in all things they were to be subject to their Bishop.

These conclusions are in no way affected by the case of the Chorepiscopi (or country Bishops). The title ' Chorepiscopus' first occurs in the 13th Canon of the Council of Ancyra (a small Council of 18 Bishops, held A.D. 314). This Canon enacts that, " Chorepiscopi shall not ordain Priests or Deacons, still less shall they ordain city Priests, except by written leave from the Bishop in each Diocese." * Who were these Chorepiscopi, and what were their duties? The Chorepiscopus was the Vicegerent of the city Bishop, and acted for him in confirming the baptized, in presiding over the country clergy, enquiring into their behaviour and making report thereof to the city Bishop, and in ordaining the clergy of the minor orders, such as Readers, Sub-deacons, &c., and sometimes by special license from the city Bishop, the Presbyters, and Deacons. † But to what order did he belong? Was he merely equivalent to a rural Dean, or was he a duly consecrated Bishop? If we take into consideration *the object of his appointment*, he may have been, and that too without any encroachment upon what we have seen was held to be the prerogative of the first Order, viz., ordination, either a Bishop, or a Presbyter, according to the duties which he had to perform. In some cases where the city Bishop did not need the help of the Chorepiscopus in ordaining, a Presbyter may have sufficed for the office. In other cases, it may have been expedient that he should be a Bishop—and indeed there are historical instances where he actually was so. (*Bingham*, Book II., Sect. iii.) But if we take into consideration the *name*,

---

* The following is the text as given in Routh's Rell. Sac. IV., 214 :—

Χωρεπισκόποις μὴ ἐζεῖναι πρεσβυτέρους ἢ διακόνους χειροτονεῖν, ἀλλὰ μὴν μηδὲ πρεσβυτέρους πόλεως, χωρὶς τοῦ ἐτιτραπῆναι ὑπὸ τοῦ ἐπισκόπου μετὰ γραμμάτων, ἐν ἑκάστῃ παροικίᾳ.

The Latin Version gives a different interpretation from what we have done :—" Chorepiscopis non licere presbyteros aut diaconos ordinare ; sed nec presbyteris civitatis, sine præcepto episcopi vel litteris, in unaquaque parochiâ. [Adjectum est, *aliquid imperare, nec sine auctoritate litterarum ejus, in unaquaque parochia aliquid agere.*]

Agreeable to this version, Johnson (*Vade Mecum*) translates :—" 'Tis not allowed that a Village-Bishop do ordain Priests or Deacons ; nor that the Priests that are in every parish do anything without the license of the Bishop in writing."

But Bright (*Church History*, p. 6), following the Greek text, translates as we have done above, and says that this Canon " forbids an inferior class of consecrated Bishops, named *Chorepiscopi*, to ordain Priests or Deacons, except by written leave from the Bishops."

Whichever of these two translations we follow, it will be seen that Mr. Sprott has no grounds for saying (*Sermon*, p. 22) that this Canon admits the right of Presbyters to ordain, unless indeed he can prove that *all* the Chorepiscopi belonged to the *second* order. But so far from belonging to the *second* order, we have shown grounds for believing that they *all* belonged to the *first* order.

† *Bingham*, Book II., Sections vi. and vii.

all Chorepiscopi (*i.e.,* country Bishops) probably belonged to the *first order.* This is the opinion of Bingham. " And there needs," he writes, "no fuller proof of this than what Athanasius says in his 2nd Apology, where he puts a manifest distinction betwixt Presbyters and Chorepiscopi. For, speaking of the irregular promotion of Ischyras, who was made Bishop of the Region of Mareotis by the Eusebian faction, he says Mareotis was only a Region of Alexandria, and that all the Churches of that Precinct were immediately subject to the Bishop of Alexandria, and had never either Bishop or Chorepiscopus among them, but only Presbyters, fixt each in their respective villages or Churches. This shows evidently that the Chorepiscopi were not the same with Presbyters, however the Forger of the Decretal Epistles, under the name of Pope Leo and Damasus, would have persuaded the world to believe so." (Book II., Sect. iv.)

The Representative, then, of the Chorepiscopus in modern times is not the rural Dean, but the Bishop Suffragan.

THE PRE-REFORMATION PERIOD.

We now come to the period when the Church was politically established under Constantine, the first Christian Emperor. In his reign, the first General Council met at Nicæa, A.D. 325. At this Council there were 318 Bishops present, who, among other things, enacted a number of Canons on ecclesiastical jurisdiction, one of which expressly ordained, that " neither Priests nor Deacons shall be received into another Church without the consent of their Bishop" (Can. 16); and another, that " there shall not be two Bishops in one city. " (Can. 8.)

But it would be superfluous to pursue our Catena of Authorities further. For 1500 years, without interruption, the threefold ministry of Bishops, Presbyters, and Deacons, was the only ministry to be found in the Christian Church throughout the whole world. Instead, therefore, of continuing our Catena, we propose in this and the following Periods, to confine our attention to objections to a three-fold ministry, or what may be more aptly described as *the exceptions which prove the rule.*

1.—AERIUS.

Aerius, a Presbyter of the Church of Sebaste, in the fourth century, was one of these exceptions. Having been disappointed in his aspirations to the Bishopric of Sebaste, he declared " that Bishops and Presbyters were altogether equal, and that a Presbyter could ordain as well as a Bishop." But so great was the outcry of the whole Church against these sentiments, as to show that no other form of Church government but Episcopacy had ever been heard of before. It was then the settled doctrine of the Catholic Church that Bishops excel Presbyters, "inasmuch as the order of Bishops can beget Fathers to the Church by ordination, but the order of Presbyters can but beget sons by baptism." (*Epiphanius, Hæres.*, 75.)

2.—ISCHYRAS.

The practice of the early Church is seen again in the case of Ischyras who was ordained by a mere Presbyter named Colluthus. Whilst the Presbyters ordained by Meletius, a schismatical Bishop, were received into the Church as Presbyters, without undergoing re-ordination ; Ischyras was treated as if a mere layman, having received his orders from one who had no power to give them. (*Theophilus Anglicanus,* p. 102.)

3 —HILARY, CHRYSOSTOM, JEROME, AND EUTYCHIUS.

There are also certain writers and Fathers of the 4th century, and a Patriarch of the 10th, quoted by Presbyterians and other upholders of parity, as favouring their views. But as we have already traced Episcopacy down to the present time (the 4th century), and no other form of Church Government has been heard of, and as these Fathers and writers testify to the existence of a threefold ministry in their own days, we might on *a priori* grounds safely pass by their alleged testimony in favour of parity in Church Government, as at best only *opinions* and not *facts*. However let us examine the nature of the so-called Anti-Episcopal evidence.

a.—Hilary the Deacon is one of those usually quoted as Anti-Episcopal. The following passages are given :—

" He calls Timothy, made by him a Presbyter, Bishop, because at first Presbyters were called Bishops ; that one ceasing, the next in order might succeed him. Finally, in Egypt, Presbyters confirm if the Bishop is not present. But because the Presbyters next in order began to be found unworthy of holding the primacy, the mode was changed; the Council seeing that not order but merit should make a Bishop, appointed by the choice of many Priests, lest an unworthy person should rashly usurp [the office], and become a stumbling-block to many." (*Comment. on Eph.* iv., 11.)

And, "after the Bishop, however, he places the ordination of a Deacon. Wherefore? Unless that the ordination of a Bishop and a Presbyter is the same. For each is a Priest; but the Bishop is first; inasmuch as every Bishop is a Presbyter, but not every Presbyter a Bishop; for he is a Bishop who is first amongst the Presbyters." (*Comment on 1 Tim.* iii. 10.)

As Hilary here evidently states merely his own private opinion, deduced from the language of St. Paul, and when we remember that he joined himself to one of the most violent men of those days, the schismatic Lucifer of Cagliari, and that he held such extreme views on baptism, that Jerome sarcastically called him "the Deucalion of the world," we cannot regard the passages quoted as having any weight in the controversy. We must not accept Hilary's *private opinions* in opposition to the *testimony* of the *whole* Church. Besides, if it is allowable for Presbyterians to quote one class of passages from him, surely Episcopalians are in all fairness entitled to quote a different class—for instance, the passage in which he says that in "a Church there are several Presbyters or Deacons, but never more than one Bishop, even in Apostolic times. Because all things are from God the Father, *He decreed* that each Church should be *governed* by one Bishop." (*Comment. on 1 Cor.* xii. 28.) Or, again, "In the Bishop *are all the orders*, because he is the prince of Priests." (*Comment. on Eph.* iv. 11.) And again, those passages in which he tells us that Timothy and Titus, and the Angels of the Apocalyptic Churches were Bishops. (*Pearson, Vindic. Ignat.*, Part II., Chap. xiii.)

b.—Chrysostom [A.D. 347-407] is also sometimes brought forward as an Anti-Episcopal authority. One would have thought that the history of his own Episcopal actions would alone have been sufficient to prevent any such charge being brought against him. * But even the very passage quoted by the opponents of Episcopacy is of itself sufficient to show that

---

* See *Hooker's Eccl. Polity*, Book vii., Chap. 6.

Chrysostom was no Anti-Episcopalian; for it distinctly says (and this is the great point in question) that the Bishop had a power, with which the Presbyters were not entrusted, viz., the power of ordination. "The reason"—he says, in his eleventh homily on the first epistle to Timothy—"the reason why the Apostle, having delivered rules for the behaviour of Bishops, immediately proceeds to the Deacons, without mentioning the intermediate order of Presbyters, was this, that there was not *a great difference* between them and Bishops; for even Presbyters are entrusted to teach, and to preside in the Church; so that the same rules which are prescribed for Bishops may also serve for Presbyters: a Bishop can discharge no function, *except imposition of hands*, which may not be exercised by Presbyters." *

c.—Jerome [A.D. 345-420] is another presumed Anti-Episcopalian. And since he is quoted as an authority by the opponents of Episcopacy, it is to be hoped they will accept all that he says about the three orders. He writes:—"That which Aaron, and his sons, and the Levites, were in the Temple, that let the Bishops, and Presbyters, and Deacons claim to be in the Church" (*Ep.* 101 *to Evang.*) Again, "Neither the pomp of riches, nor the lowliness of poverty, makes a Bishop greater or less: all alike are successors of the Apostles." (*Ep. ad Evang.* 101.) Also, "With us the Bishops hold the place of the Apostles" (*Ad Marcellam*, Ep. 5). A Presbyter, he says, cannot ordain. (*Ep. ad Evang.* 101.) Against the Luciferians he argues that "the safety of the Church depends on the dignity of the Chief Priest [or Bishop], to whom, if a peculiar power be not given, superior to that of others, there will be as many schisms as Priests in the Churches. Hence it is that, without the command of the Bishop, neither a Presbyter nor a Deacon can baptize. The Bishop is to impose his hands on those who have been baptized by Presbyters and Deacons, for the invocation of the Holy Spirit." In his *Catalogue of Ecclesiastical Writers* he mentions "St. James the Just, called the brother of our Lord, as ordained by the Apostles, Bishop of Jerusalem, Timothy, as ordained Bishop of Ephesus by St. Paul, and Polycarp, Bishop of Smyrna by St. John." Now, surely no passage in Jerome's writings is to be read so as to contradict these clear statements, and also the unanimous voice of antiquity.

* *Sinclair's Vindication*, p. 65.

One of the passages which is usually quoted against Epis-copacy is the following :—" Before the time came when divisions in religion by the instigation of the devil began, and cries were raised among the people, ' I am of Paul ; I am of Apollos ; and I of Cephas," the Churches were governed by a Joint-Council of Presbyters. But afterwards (when each Presbyter considered those disciples whom he had baptized to be his own, and not Christ's), *it was decreed over all the world* that one Presbyter chosen from his brethren should be ap-pointed over the rest, on whom the whole management of the Church should devolve ; and by these means the seeds of schism be removed." (*Comment. on Titus* i.)

It is to be observed that Jerome gives no authority for this statement. It is evidently nothing more than his own private inference from Scripture. And we are just as much entitled as was Jerome (who was not born till the middle of the fourth century) to draw our own inferences from Scripture. Besides, in the sense in which the opponents of Episcopacy read the passage, they make Jerome to contradict himself in those passages mentioned before And after all, his words are not capable of bearing the construction which they seek to attach to them. They cannot by any possibility be twisted round to imply that the Episcopal order was not instituted till towards the middle of the second century. " We do not deny that in the Apostolic age, the names Bishops and Presbyters were applied to the same persons ; but *then*, there were at that time *Bishops* also, in our sense of the word, namely, the *Holy Apostles* themselves : and (whatever may be alleged as the *reason* for the institution of Episcopacy) the *fact* and *time* of its institution are the only questions with which we are concerned. Now in this very passage St. Jerome testifies that " it was decreed *over all the world*, that one Presbyter chosen from his brethren should be appointed over the rest, on whom the whole management of the Church should devolve." And that which was received throughout *the whole world*, and of which the *origin does not appear* (and which Jerome himself seems to ascribe to the age of Apollos and Cephas, that is, to the *Apostolic* age, and, in the case of St. James, does, as we have seen, make immediately consequent on our Lord's Ascension), could not be of *human* institution, if it were only from the rule of St. Augustine, " That which is *held* by the *Universal Church* (as St. Jerome says is the case with *Episcopacy*), and not ordained by any *Council* (and Councils all *presuppose Bishops*, for they *consist* of them), but has always been retained in the Church, is to be believed to have come down from Apostolical authority." *

But the upholders of parity in Church Government go on to quote from Jerome (*Ep.* 101 *to Evang.*) in illustration of the practice which they say had long subsisted at Alexandria, that "from the days of St. Mark the Evangelist, down to those of the Bishops Heraclas and Dionysius, the Presbyters of Alexandria always nominated as Bishop, one chosen from among themselves, and placed in a higher grade, as an army would make an Emperor, or Deacons choose an Archdeacon." But why should they drop the quotation here ? We Episcopalians are not afraid of Jerome, so let us continue it. He adds, " For what doth a Bishop do, *ordination excepted*, which a Presbyter may not do ? " But here is granted the whole point in question, and we now see why our opponents usually do not care to give the full quotation. As well might they prove from the Bible "there is no God," by omitting the words, " the fool hath said in his heart," as disprove Episcopacy from this passage of Jerome. But " the drift and purpose of St. Jerome's speech doth plainly show what his meaning was ; for whereas some did over-extol the office of the Deacon in the Church of Rome, where Deacons being grown great through wealth, challenged place above Presbyters ; St. Jerome, to abate this insolency, writing to Evangelus, diminisheth by all means the Deacons' estimation, and lifteth up Presbyters as far as possible the truth might bear."† And being a man of a hot temper, his language was not of the most guarded kind. Still, at the utmost, that language cannot mean more than that the Alexandrian Presbyters till the days of Heraclas and Dionysius had the privilege of nominating their Bishop out of their own order, the nominee being afterwards Episcopally ordained. But even some, *e.g.*, Pearson, tell us that the passage does not imply so much ; that it merely says the Bishop was nominated '*from*' the College of their own Presbyters, and not from abroad or from an inferior order of Clergy, but that it is not said he was nominated ' *by* ' the Presbyters. Whichever of these two is

---

* *Theophilus Anglicanus*, p. 92.

† *Hooker's Eccl. Pol.*, Book VII., Chap. 5.

the proper interpretation, one thing is certain, " that generally of regiment by Bishops, and what term of continuance it had in the Church of Alexandria, it was no part of Jerome's mind to speak." *

d.—Eutychius, Patriarch of Alexandria, according to the opponents of Episcopacy, improves upon Jerome's story " by taking notice of the same practice with greater particularity of circumstances." He says that "Mark appointed twelve Presbyters who should remain with the Patriarch, so that when the Patriarchate became vacant they might choose one from the twelve Presbyters, on whose head the remaining eleven might place their hands, and bless him, and make him Patriarch. Nor did this institution concerning the Presbyters cease at Alexandria, namely, that they should make the Patriarchs from the twelve Presbyters, until the time of Alexander, the Patriarch of Alexandria, who was the 318th of that number. He, however, forbade that the Presbyters should make the Patriarch in future, and decreed that, on the death of the Patriarch, the Bishops should assemble for the purpose of ordaining a Patriarch."

Now, with regard to this passage, it is well to remember that Eutychius " lived as far down as the *tenth* century, and though a Patriarch, such as the Church produced at that day, was remarkable for nothing so much as his credulity, and the inconsistency of his narratives, not only with those of more authentic histories, but often with themselves." † He gives no authorities for his statements here, and surely if such an anomalous practice had existed at Alexandria, as the opponents of Episcopacy would fain seek to establish, Clement and Origen, who both belonged to that Church, and lived at the time to which Eutychius refers, would have taken some notice of it. We are not to receive against all early ecclesiastical writers, Eutychius, a man continually at variance with the people committed to his charge, ‡ and who had no better, probably less, means of information than we have,—the Alexandrian library with all its early records having been burned by the Mahometans about 200 years before his time. Besides, there is a discrepancy of nearly 100 years between

---

* *Hooker's Eccl. Pol.*, Book VII., Chap. 5.

† *Bp. Skinner's Primitive Truth and Order*, p. 298.

‡ *Pearson Vindic. Ingat.*, Part I., Chap. XI., § II.

the date given by him and that given by Jerome, as the termination of the alleged peculiar practice at Alexandria. And, whereas Jerome merely says that the Presbyters having placed the person chosen "in a higher seat named him Bishop," but makes no mention of ordination; Eutychius "improves" upon this, and adds that "they placed their hands on his head, blessed him, and made him Patriarch." But Eutychius evidently imputes the practice of his own age to an earlier one when there were no Patriarchs in the Alexandrian Church in the special sense of the word, and thus by an egregious blunder comes to attribute the laying on of hands, which was performed by Bishops alone to the Presbyters who nominated the Bishop. Surely Eutychius, who manifestly commits this error, is not to be believed in preference to that other account which has come down to us from a much earlier period than that in which Eutychius lived—namely, from the very times of which he speaks. In the Apostolic Constitutions we read (B. vii., chap. 46), that of the Bishops of Alexandria "Annianus was the first, ordained by Mark the Evangelist; the second, Avilius by Luke, who was also an Evangelist," that is to say, Annianus and Avilius were Episcopally ordained. The argument then which the opponents of Episcopacy seek to draw from the statement of Eutychius, when closely examined, entirely falls to the ground.

4.—THE EARLY SCOTTISH CHURCH.

The early history of the Scottish Church has also been supposed, but falsely so, to supply an argument against a threefold Ministry.

By the beginning of the third century, Christianity had found its way into Northern Britain. But Prosper Aquitanus states that "Palladius was raised to the Episcopate by Pope Celestine, and sent by him to the Scots believing in Christ, as their first Bishop." This mission of Palladius took place A.D. 431. Here, then, in Scotland, according to the opponents of Episcopacy, was a Church whose Government continued to be Presbyterian for the space of two centuries. But in this inference from Prosper's words they commit a grievous chronological error. They assume that the "Scots," to whom Palladius was sent, were the inhabitants of Northern Britain; whereas they were the inhabitants of what we now call

Ireland. As yet there was no kingdom of the Scottish race established in Britain : the only Scots of those days were the Scots of Ireland. *

The peculiar form of ecclesiastical government at Iona has also been laid hold of by the opponents of episcopacy. In the year of our Lord 563, Columba sailed from Ireland and landed in Iona. There he established a monastery of which he continued Abbot till the day of his death. Other monastries were in the course of time established on the model of that at Iona, to which they were all subject. Thus the Abbot of Iona was the superior of the whole Columbite family. But he could not by the very tenure of his office be a Bishop; he must of necessity be a Presbyter. Because Columba himself was merely a Presbyter and not a Bishop, no Bishop could sit in Columba's chair. And this rule was invariably observed during the whole of the primacy of Iona, *i.e.*, down to the middle of the ninth century.

There would, however, be nothing strange in this, had the Abbots of Iona been merely the superiors of the Columbite order ; but they were also Primates of the Picts and Scots. Owing to the personal influence of Columba, and as a recompense for his great services, this primacy was vested in him and his successors. Must we suppose then that the order of Bishops was unknown amongst the Picts and Scots during this time ? Nay : they were in communion with Churches that had Bishops—no Church in fact was then without them—and thus so far from the order of Bishops being unknown to them they were themselves likely to have had them. Indeed, we know that they did have them, for persons were known amongst the Columbites as Bishops, they were raised to that degree, and some of those so raised were sent to the English. But might they not, although called Bishops, have had only Presbyterian orders ? Not so, for those sent to England were recognised by others who undoubtedly had preserved the Apostolical succession, as *possessing all the powers which belong to the Episcopal order.* That the superiority of a Bishop over a Presbyter was recognized even by the Columbites themselves, is evident from the record which has come down to us of the visit of Cronan, Bishop of Munster, to Columba at Iona. The Bishop out of humility concealed his Episcopal

* *Grub's. Eccl. Hist. of Scotland*, Vol. i., p. 25.

character, and was thought to be only a Presbyter. But the real state of the matter became known to Columba, and he asked his guest to consecrate the Eucharist. Cronan in turn requested Columba to assist in breaking the bread, as if both were merely Presbyters, but Columba replied:—"Christ bless you, my brother. Do you alone, as a Bishop, break the bread according to the episcopal rite, now we know that you are a Bishop. Wherefore have you hitherto laboured to conceal yourself from us, and so hindered us from yielding the reverence which is your due?"

Another incident of those times shows that ordination was the prerogative of the Episcopal order. One of Columba's disciples, the Presbyter Findchan, Abbot of Artchain, was desirous to have Aidus, a cruel and wicked man, whose hands were stained with blood, but for whom he had a great affection, ordained a Presbyter. The Bishop sent for refused to ordain such a man, unless Findchan would also, in confirmation of the act, lay his hands along with him on Aidus' head. Findchan did so, and thus Aidus was ordained in violation of the Canons. Columba on hearing what had been done, was wroth, and pronounced judgment on Findchan for "impiously and against the law of the church" laying hands on Aidus; and on Aidus who had been "thus unlawfully ordained." This narrative of Adamnan's distinctly shows that it was not lawful for a Presbyter to ordain. For if it had, Findchan, who was bent on his friend being raised to the priesthood, would not have requested another to ordain the murderer Aidus, when he had every reason to expect a refusal. He would have ordained him himself.

With regard to ordination then, we may confidently affirm that in the early Scottish Church, the rule was that *Bishops alone* had this prerogative. It was only as regards jurisdiction that any irregularity existed. * But in so far as the Ecclesiastical system differed from the rule of the Universal Church,

* Modern parallels of the system at Iona have been frequently pointed out, *e.g.*, "A Bishop holding a canonry in a Cathedral, where, as one of the chapter, he is inferior to the Dean ; or possessing an office in a Univer- and being in that capacity subordinate to the Chancellor and Vice-Chan- cellor." "Even down to the year 1752 the Presbyter-Abbot of the great monastery of Fulda had under him a Bishop, for the purpose of ordina- tion, and other Episcopal functions."

But see *Grub's Ecclesiastical History of Scotland*, Vol. i., p. 137, which we have followed throughout in our remarks above.

it was necessarily *imperfect*, and so forms no precedent for future ages.

5.—THE WALDENSES.

The Waldenses (otherwise called the Vaudois, Vallenses) a primitive people inhabiting the valleys of the Cottian Alps, and receiving their name from their abode, are also urged, but without any just grounds, as an exception to the rule which we have laid down with regard to the universal prevalence of a three-fold Ministry for the first fifteen centuries after the foundation of the Christian Church. The exception taken arises, however, from a misapprehension. It is made on the supposition that the Waldenses had their title and origin from Peter Waldo, a native of Lyons, who was excommunicated as a heretic by the Archbishop of that place, A.D. 1172, and of whom no mention is made before A.D. 1160. But there is evidence that the Waldenses existed as a distinct society at least fifty years previous to this date; and it is probable that the Subalpini and Paterines, a more ancient name still, was but a prior designation of these same Waldenses. Certain it is that there is not the slightest shadow of proof that Peter Waldo ever visited Piedmont; and it is known that there exists this difference between his followers and the Church of the Alps, that whilst they *assumed all the functions of the clerical office without any direct appointment*, the Church of the Alps insisted upon a regular call and ordination for its ministers. Indeed the form of Church Government among the Waldenses was *Episcopal*, until in the 17th century, a dreadful pestilence which left but two out of thirteen pastors surviving, rendered it necessary to seek aid from Switzerland. Naturally enough there was sent back to the Waldenses the Presbyterian form of Government, and the Genevan Liturgy. But previous to this time, Episcopacy prevailed. *

C.—THE REFORMATION PERIOD.

I.—In this period we hear for the first time of any systematic violation of the Church's rule with regard to Episcopal

* On the subject of the Waldenses, see *Blunt's Reformation in England*, p. 77; also, *Mosheim's Church History*, edited by Dr. Maclaine, Vol. i., p. 304, n. 6.

Ordination. But that this violation was originally the result of necessity rather than of choice—however much the necessity may have been afterwards magnified into a virtue, and the violation made on deliberate purpose—will be seen from the following statements from the leading Reformers in those Churches in which the Apostolical Succession was lost.

1. The Augsburg Confession, which Calvin says he willingly and heartily subscribed, expresses the *Lutheran* view of the matter. "Now here again we desire to testify to the world that we would willingly preserve the Ecclesiastical and Canonical government, if the Bishops would only cease to exercise cruelty upon our Churches. This our desire will excuse us before God, before all the world, and unto all posterity; that it may not be justly imputed to us that the authority of Bishops is impaired amongst us; when men shall hear and read that we, earnestly deprecating the unjust cruelty of the Bishops, could obtain no equal measure at their hands." *

2. *Grotius*, by birth and education a Presbyterian, may be regarded as the exponent of the views of the *Arminians*. He writes, "That Episcopacy was received by the *Universal Church* is evident from the *General Councils;* is evident also from the gathering together of Synods both national and provincial. *All the Fathers without a single exception* bear witness to the pre-eminence of Bishops, and he of them who pays least deference to the Episcopal office is Jerome; yet his testimony is sufficient, "It was decreed *over all the world,*" &c.† That Episcopacy had its beginning in the Apostolic times, the catalogues of Bishops in Irenæus, Eusebius, and Socrates bear witness. That Episcopacy is of approved Divine right, the Divine Apocalypse bears an irrefragable argument." . . . "When it is asked whether Episcopacy is of Divine right, it is sufficient to reply that Christ gave the model of that form of government in the appointment of the College of Apostles; that this model was followed by the Apostles, and has been most manifestly adhered to by the Universal Church, with the exception of a few innovators of our own days."‡

* Quoted in *Theophilus Anglicanus,* p. 104.

† See p. 36.

‡ Grotius quoted in *Theophilus Anglicanus,* p. 93.

Grotius thus sums up the argument between the Episco-
palian writers and their opponents in his time. "So light
and foolish is what the latter have put forth in answer to the
former, that to have read the one is to have already refuted
the other; especially touching the Angels of the Churches,
concerning whom, that which the disturbers of ecclesiastical
order bring, is so absurd and contrary to the sacred text
itself, that it deserves not confutation" (*Discussio de Primatu
Papœ*).

It were to be wished that Grotius's exhortation to the
Reformed Churches might find a responsive echo in our day.
He advises them to appoint certain of themselves to occupy
the higher degree of Bishops, and to procure proper Episcopal Ordination for them, "and that those so ordained should
in their turn ordain other Pastors, and in this way the
beginning be made of a return to the old and healthy
customs; by the despising of which, licence has run riot in
forming new Churches in accordance with new opinions, and
what they are to believe in the course of a few years, we
know not." (*Ep.*, p. 975.)

3. Having listened to the Lutheran and Arminian statements, let us now listen to the *Genevan*, of which *Calvin* shall
be the exponent. He writes :—

"We do not deny that we have not such a discipline
as the ancient Church had—but what justice is there in our
being accused of having a subverted discipline, by those who
entirely deprived us of it? *Episcopacy proceeded from God;
the office of Bishop was appointed by the authority of God*, and
defined by laws." (*Ep. ad Cardinal Sadolet.*)

Again, "If they would give us an hierarchy, in which the
Bishops did so rise above others, as that they would not
refuse to be subject to Christ, and to depend on Him as their
only Head, and be referred to Him; in which they would so
preserve brotherly union among themselves, as to be united
by nothing so much as His truth, then indeed I should confess, that those persons are deserving of every the severest
anathema, if any such there be, who would not reverence
such an hierarchy, and submit to it with the utmost obedience."
(*De Necess. Reform. Eccles.*)

Calvin's dictum is well known—"Parity breedeth confusion."

4. But this Ecclesiastical axiom of Calvin brings us to our

own country, and to *Knox*, who also with Calvin had to confess that "parity is the mother of confusion." John Knox himself, as may be seen from his adoption of this axiom, was no favourer of that parity of ministers which Andrew Melville afterwards introduced, but may be looked upon as, more or less, a witness for the distinction between Bishops and Presbyters. * So far from being the father of Presbyterianism he contributed towards the establishment in Scotland of Superintendents, which is but the Latin name for Bishops, and who in every respect, Ordination excepted, were Bishops. As a further proof of his leaning towards Episcopacy may be mentioned the facts, that he officiated for some years 'as a Clergyman of the Church of England both at Berwick and at Newcastle, and that he was Chaplain to King Edward VI., at a time when, as now, the Preface to the Ordinal declared: "It is evident unto all men dilligently reading the holy Scripture and ancient Authors, that from the Apostles' time there have been these Orders of Ministers in Christ's Church: Bishops Priests, and Deacons." Of this Episcopal partiality the family of Knox gave hereditary proof by becoming members and Clergymen of the Church of England. †

II.—Such are the views of the Continental Reformers, and of Knox in Scotland, with regard to Episcopacy. Let us now see what is the mind of the Anglican Church on the subject. And this we shall ascertain by referring to her Articles and Formularies and comparing them one with another.

1. Article XIX. defines " the visible Church of Christ " to be " a congregation of faithful men, in the which the pure Word of God is preached, and the Sacraments be duly ministered, according to Christ's ordinance in all those things that of necessity are requisite to the same." We are not here told what things are " requisite," but if we turn to Article XXIII., we find it there stated that, " It is not lawful for any man to take upon him the office of public preaching, or ministering the Sacraments in the Congregation, before he be lawfully called, and sent to execute the same. And those we ought to judge lawfully called and sent, which be chosen and called to this work by men who have public authority

---

* See *Harington's Notes on the Church of Scotland.*

† *Stephen's History of the Reformation in Scotland,* p. 161.

given unto them in the Congregation, to call and send ministers into the Lord's vineyard."

We have thus advanced a step further, but still we have to ascertain who those are who have this authority of calling and sending ministers. From Article XXVI. we learn indeed that those to whom is committed "the ministration of the Word and Sacraments," "do not the same in their own name, but in Christ's, and do minister by His commission and authority;" but the question remains, through whom does Christ grant this commission? If we turn to Article XXXVI. we read that, "The Book of Consecration of Archbishops and Bishops, and ordering of Priests and Deacons, . . . doth contain all things necessary to such Consecration and Ordering; neither hath it anything that of itself is superstitious or ungodly." This Article sends us to the Ordinal, and there we find these distinct and striking words (which have been assigned to Cranmer):—"It is evident unto all men diligently reading the Holy Scripture and ancient Authors, that from the Apostles' time there have been these Orders of Ministers in Christ's Church; Bishops, Priests, and Deacons. Which Offices were evermore had in such reverend Estimation, that no man might presume to execute any of them, except he were first called, tried, examined, and known to have such qualities as are requisite for the same; and also by publick Prayer, with Imposition of Hands, were approved and admitted thereunto by lawful authority. And therefore, to the intent that these Orders may be continued, and reverently used and esteemed, in the United Church of England and Ireland; no man shall be accounted or taken to be a lawful Bishop, Priest, or Deacon in the United Church of England and Ireland, or suffered to execute any of the said Functions, except he be called, tried, examined, and admitted thereunto, according to the Form hereafter following, or *hath had formerly Episcopal Consecration, or Ordination.*"

These last words, coupled with the fact that a clergyman of the Roman Church is, on abjuring his errors, admitted to officiate in the Church of England without re-ordination; whilst Presbyterian and other Ministers of parity are treated in all respects as laymen, and have to submit to re-ordination before being allowed to officiate within her pale,* show that it is not a legal qualification which is referred to, but a purely

* *Farquhar's Prelacy, not Presbytery,* p. 13.

spiritual one, "derived from Christ Himself, through the only visible channel which He has Himself appointed." *

2. But the strength of a chain is only equal to that of its weakest link. Hence, if a single link in the Apostolical Succession of our branch of the Catholic Church be broken, all her clergy are cut off from that Succession. If the Series was ever interrupted, the Ordinal † ensures that it could only have been at the time of the Reformation. Was the Succession of the Episcopal Order then continued without interruption, or was it not? The Nag's Head Story says that it was not. But this story has been again and again " proved to be a late invented, inconsistent, self-contradictory, and absurd fable." ‡ Perhaps the best and fullest refutation of it is to be found in Archbishop Bramhall's Works (p. 436), " They say that Archbishop Parker and the rest of the Protestant Bishops in the beginning of Queen Elizabeth's reign, or at least sundry of them, were consecrated at the Nag's Head in Cheapside, together, by Bishop Scory alone, or by him and Bishop Barlow, without sermon, without sacrament, without solemnity, in the year 1559 (but they know not what day nor before what public notaries), by a new phantastic form. And all this they, on the supposed voluntary report of Mr. Neale (a single malicious spy) in private to his own party, long after the business pretended to be done."

* *Woodgate's Historical Sermons*, p. 308.

† " It has been objected that the Bishops consecrated according to the Ordinal of Edward VI. and Elizabeth, could not have been rightly consecrated, because the words of consecration were only, 'Take the Holy Ghost, and remember that thou stir up the grace of God which is in thee by the imposition of hands ; for God hath not given us the Spirit of fear, but of power, of love, and soberness.' Here is nothing which might not apply to a Priest or Deacon, as well as to a Bishop."

" But we may reply that the whole service concerns Bishops, not Priests and Deacons ; and that, if the words, ' for the office of a Bishop,' &c., afterwards inserted, were not at first added, it is quite evident that they were sufficiently implied. Everybody must have felt that it was episcopal consecration which was conferred. The form of ordination does not consist merely in the prayer of consecration. The whole service forms part of it. And, moreover, even in the Roman Pontifical, the words which accompany the imposition of hands are simply, ' Receive the Holy Ghost'; and the prayer, which follows, does not directly mention the office of a Bishop."—*Browne's Exposition of the XXXIX. Articles*, p. 782.

‡ T. Browne, quoted in *Theophilus Anglicanus*, p. 209.

"We say that Archbishop Parker was consecrated alone at Lambeth, in the Church, by four Bishops, authorised thereunto by commission under the great seal of England, with sermon, with sacrament, with due solemnities, on the 17th day of December, anno 1559, before four of the most eminent public notaries in England, and particularly the same public notary was principal actuary, both at Cardinal Pole's consecration, and Archbishop Parker's. And that all the rest of the Bishops were consecrated at other times, some in the same month, but not upon the same day, some in the same year, but not the same month, and some the year following. And to prove the truth of our relation, and falsehood of theirs, we produce the register of the See of Canterbury, as authentic as the world hath any, the registers of the other fourteen sees then vacant, all as carefully kept by sworn officers, as the records of the Vatican itself. We produce all the commissions under the Privy Seal and Great Seal of England. We produce the rolls and records of the Chancery, and if the records of the Signet Office had not been unfortunately burned in King James' time, it might have been verified by them also. We produce an Act of Parliament, express to the point, within seven years after the consecration; we produce all the controverted consecrations published to the world in print, anno 1572, three years before Archbishop Parker's death; whilst all things were fresh in men's memories."

There is not the slightest ground then for questioning the validity of Anglican Orders. Even Romanists are obliged to bear testimony to this fact. *

3. The present succession in the Scottish Episcopal Church is derived through the Church of England. In early days, Scotland sent Bishops to England, but in later times England has had to repay this debt. Twice has the Apostolical succession been lost in Scotland. On the first of these occasions it was renewed by the consecration of the Archbishop of Glasgow, and the Bishops of Brechin and Galloway, by the Bishops of London, Ely, Rochester, and Worcester, These Prelates were consecrated at London, on Sunday, 21st October, 1610, according to the form in the English Ordinal, only it was not deemed necessary that they should pass through the intermediate orders of Deacon and Priest. †

* For a list of testimonies see *Theophilus Anglicanus*, p 210.
† *Grub's Eccles. Hist. of Scotland*, Vol. II., p. 296.

But the succession thus renewed, was again lost in the troublesome times which followed the accession of Charles the First to the throne. The Scottish Bishops were driven into exile, and all, with the exception of one, died, without being able to provide for the Episcopal succession. Accordingly recourse had to be made a second time to the English Church. Four persons were nominated for the Scottish Episcopate, and sent to London for consecration. There, James Sharp was consecrated Archbishop of S. Andrew's, Andrew Fairfoul, Archbishop of Glasgow, Robert Leighton, Bishop of Dumblane, and James Hamilton, Bishop of Galloway, on 15th December, 1661, in S. Peter's, Westminster, by the Bishops of London, Worcester, Carlisle, and Landaff. But on neither of these two occasions did either of the two Archbishops officiate, lest their doing so might seem to imply that they claimed a superiority over the Scottish Church. One thing however there is, which distinguishes the latter from the former consecration. Whereas in the former, the persons sent to London were raised to the Episcopate at once, without passing through the intermediate stages of Deacon and Priest, it was not so done on this occasion. Fairfoul and Hamilton had been raised to the priesthood by the Scottish Bishops of the old succession, and so were consecrated Bishops at once; but Sharp and Leighton, being only in Presbyterian orders, had to submit to re-ordination, and were each regularly ordained Deacon and Priest before being advanced to the Episcopate. *

Thus was the Apostolical Succession a second time restored to Scotland; nor has it ever since been lost. †

---

* *Grub's Eccles. Hist. of Scotland*, Vol. III., p. 195.

† Mr Sprott in his *Exclusive Right of Presbyters to Ordain* (p. 19), endeavours to invalidate the Orders of the Scottish Episcopal Church by stating that when Episcopacy was disestablished in Scotland, two of the three Bishops who continued the Episcopal Succession "had no ordination as Presbyters except what they had received from Presbyteries." But, granting the truth of this statement, the fact of their being raised to the Episcopate, *per saltum*, without passing through the intermediate stages, does not invalidate, but only render irregular, their consecration. However, our Scottish Bishops can all trace up their Orders through the third Bishop (Alexander Rose, Bishop of Edinburgh), who was regularly consecrated after having passed through the intermediate stages of Deacon and Priest. The various links of the chain are given in the Appendix to *Skinner's Primitive Truth and Order Vindicated.* Hence

III.—CONCLUSION.

We have now reached the end of our inquiry into the history of the Christian Ministry. We have searched Scripture, and we have searched Church History, and the result of our investigations is that we find that in and from the times of the Apostles there have been in the Church of Christ three orders * of Ministers—the same three which are to be found at the present day in the Anglican branch of the Catholic Church, under the names of Bishops, Priests, and Deacons. We further find that down to the time of the Reformation, none but the members of the first order were permitted to ordain in any part of the world. † And the principle on

there can be no question about the validity of the Orders of the present occupants of the Episcopal bench in the Scottish Church. It is no real objection to their validity, that some of their predecessors in office were Bishops, "at large" and not of any particular diocese. For, as Dr. Potter in his *Discourses on Church Government* (p. 452) says, "we must carefully distinguish between the ordination of ministers, and their designation to particular districts. For these are things wholly different, though they often went together ; it being manifest, that one may be a Bishop, or Priest, where he has no authority to exercise his office ; which is the case not only of those who are ordained to convert heathens, without any title to a particular Church, but all others who travel beyond the limits of their own district : for a Priest who comes into a foreign country, where other lawful ministers are settled, still retains his sacerdotal character, and yet has no authority to take upon him the ordinary exercise of his office there."

* Throughout we have spoken of three *orders*. But it is to be observed that just as the distinction between a Priest and a Levite was greater than that between the High Priest and a Priest ; so the distinction between a Presbyter and a Deacon has always been esteemed a greater than that between a Bishop and a Presbyter—the pre-eminence of the Bishop consisting chiefly in the power of ordination. Hence, "The Fathers, the Schoolmen, and the Divines, both of the Roman and Reformed Episcopal Churches, have seemed doubtful whether Bishops and Presbyters were of different degrees in the same order, or of different orders."—*Browne's Exposition of the Thirty-nine Articles*, p. 555.

† "Those who maintain the validity of Presbyterian orders, do so on the ground that Bishops were themselves but Presbyters. Those who maintain that Episcopal ordination is necessary, reply that, even though Bishops be themselves Presbyters, yet they only, and not all Presbyters alike, had the authority to ordain ; and therefore that without them ordination could not take place. This was the constant creed of the Fathers, and of the Schoolmen after them."—*Browne's Exposition of the Thirty-nine Articles*, p. 555.

which their ordinations were deemed valid was that by regular Episcopal descent from the Apostles (to whom and their successors Christ gave His commission), they had received authority to give ordination and mission to others.

We must conclude then with Hooker (VII., V., 10)," If anything in the Church's government, surely the first institution of Bishops was from heaven, was even of God; the Holy Ghost was the author of it." Nor is the work of the Holy Spirit less observable in having guarded and preserved the Episcopal Order from the first days of the Christian Church down to the present hour. Faithfully has Christ observed His promise, " Lo, I am with you always, even to

---

" There is no example " [in the early Church] " of ordination ever being entrusted to Presbyters only." (*Ibid*, p. 553.) Mr. Sprott (*Sermon*, p. 22) imagines that he finds an example in the case of the Alexandrian Church. But it furnishes no such example, as we have already shown (pp. 28-29). His assertion that the 13th Canon of the Council of Ancyra admits the right of Presbyters to ordain, has also been distinctly shown to be unfounded.

And this fact that mere Presbyters could not ordain, coupled with that other fact which we have pointed out on p. 10 (see also *Mr. Sprott's Sermon*, pp. 8, 16), that the various orders derived their authority from above, not from below, is a sufficient answer to our opponents when they challenge us to give proof of a second ordination on the occasion of a Presbyter being raised to the Episcopal bench in the Primitive Church. For had there been no such second consecration, then either a mere Presbyter could ordain, or else the Episcopal authority did come from below not from above,—neither of which was the case.

The early Christians certainly looked upon a Bishop as something more than " first among equals, one of many Pastors appointed by the Church to take oversight of a Diocese, and in ordination, a presiding Presbyter among other Presbyters." (*Mr. Sprott's Sermon*, p. 22.) They regarded their Bishops as deriving their authority not merely from holding the priestly office, or from the bare fact of having been nominated to the Episcopate by the Clergy and people, but because they were *the consecrated Successors of the Apostles.* " We are in a position to reckon up," writes Irenæus, "those who were *by the Apostles* instituted Bishops in the Churches, and to demonstrate the successions of these men to our own times." . . . " Whom also they were leaving behind as their successors, delivering up *their own place of government to these men.*" (*Against Heresies*, B. iii., Chap. iii.) Again, S. Cyprian says that the Bishops are " the chief rulers who by *vicarious ordination* succeed to the Apostles." (*Ep.* 68.)

As a further proof of the necessity of this second ordination, we may cite the Apostolical Constitutions, which according to Bunsen represent " the life of the Church of the second and third centuries." In them it is enacted that whilst one Bishop shall be sufficient to ordain a Presbyter, there shall be three, or at least two Bishops at the consecration of a Bishop." (B. iii., §20).

the end of the world." (St. Matt. xxviii. 20.) And seeing that Episcopacy has been thus divinely instituted and preserved, surely it is an awful responsibility which they take upon themselves, who set up and follow a ministry of mere man's invention, and which was not even heard of till fifteen centuries after the Church's foundation. It is written, "no man taketh this honour to himself, but he that is called of God, as was Aaron" (Heb. v. 4); yet numbers undertake to act in God's name without being commissioned by those who alone are entitled to do so. True, they pretend to some vague sort of commission from God, but, as this alleged commission of theirs has never been substantiated by miracles (the proofs which the Apostles gave of their Divine commission), there is no reason to suppose that it is anything more than an invention to enable its claimants to get out of the difficulty of being in opposition to the practice of the Universal Church for fifteen out of eighteen centuries, and to that of nine-tenths of the modern Christian world.

We read in Jewish History of the foundation of a schismatical Church by Jeroboam. (1 Kings xii., xiii.) The worship which he set up was not necessarily idolatrous: it was fashioned after that at Jerusalem. In the temple were the Cherubim, and so Jeroboam had them also. At Jerusalem were Priests, so Jeroboam had his, but they were taken indiscriminately from all the people, and not from the appointed tribe of Levi. And because the whole system was of man's device, and not that which was Divinely instituted, God was wroth, and sent His prophet to denounce the schism. The parallel in our own country, in modern times, is obvious. But—

"Oh, rail not at our brethren of the North,
    Albeit Samaria finds her likeness there;
A self-formed Priesthood, and the Church cast forth
    To the chill mountain air.

What though their fathers sinned, and lost the grace
    Which seals the Holy Apostolic line?
Christ's love o'erflows the bounds His Prophets trace
    In His revealed design." *

The sentiment expressed in these last two lines we most heartily endorse. We believe, we trust we have proved, Episcopacy to be of Divine institution. We are confident that

* *Lyra Apostolica*, p. 141.

Christ's love flows in the channel of Episcopacy; * but God forbid that we should deny that it does not extend to those also who, by reason of their education or otherwise, have not seen fit to embrace that form of Church government. Only we trust there is no breach of charity (for, after all, truth is the greatest charity) in pointing out to them the great disadvantage they are under, in following a form of Church Government, not of Divine, but of merely human institution —in resting content with a mere peradventure, when they might have the certainty. For, if they will not use God's means, how can they expect His blessing to rest on their ways? If they will not receive the ministry which bears His commission, how can they reasonably expect Him to ratify the acts of mere self-accredited Ambassadors? Surely men do not behave so in mere worldly matters! What ambassadors of an earthly king would be received at another court, unless his credentials bore the unmistakeable impress of his master's seal? Yet why should people be less remiss about the credentials of the Ambassadors of the Heavenly King, than they are about those of the Ambassadors of some mere earthly Potentate?

But apart from the blessings of which those who reject the divinely constituted government of Episcopacy deprive themselves, there is another argument which should have much

---

* "The Church of England teaches that in the Sacraments of Baptism and the Lord's Supper are lodged certain definite gifts of God the Holy Ghost ; that in the Sacrament of Baptism is vouchsafed the first seed of a new life—the beginning of a gift of grace, which by prayer and culture will develop into the fulness of the stature of Christ ; that in the Lord's Supper the spiritual life breathed into the soul at Baptism is cherished and strengthened. It teaches again that a threefold ministry perpetuated by successive ordinations is still, as for fifteen hundred years it was never doubted to be, the divinely organised system for dispensing the Word and Sacraments. What then, it is demanded, do you cut off the grace of God from those who from various causes possess not this ministry, use not these Sacraments? Nay, the reply is in the text—"The Word of God is not bound." Not even to His Own ordinances is God's grace exclusively confined. He whose pleasure is to work by Sacraments can and does, we doubt not, work without them. I am not, therefore, called upon to water down my own creed, in tenderness to others, to hold loosely, or to preach vaguely, the doctrines of the Church to which I belong, lest I should seem to pronounce sentence on those who dissent from it, whilst I hold simultaneously with the laws of the kingdom of grace, the unlimited freedom of the action of God's word."—"*Ordination Sermons*," *by Canon Woodford.*

weight in inducing them to return to the old paths. In cutting themselves off from the Apostolical Succession, they are guilty of rending the body of Christ asunder. Schism is a very grievous sin. Of the evils which it produces there is no need to speak. They are only too patent—the bitter jealousies, heart-burnings, and strifes of the various sects, the sacrificed peace of the family circle. Schism stops the march of Christ's kingdom at home ; like a deadly enemy it tracks the footsteps of the missionary abroad.

Another evil attendant upon Schism, is the ever-increasing tendency which such an act has to repeat itself. It carries with it its own Nemesis. Once the link of the Apostolical Succession is snapped, and the Unity of the Church broken, thenceforth that party which separated itself from the rest of the body of Christ has within it the seeds of disintegration ; it is a mere heterogeneous mass, having no cohesiveness in it. The history of Presbyterianism is a proof of this. Parity has ever been, and must necessarily be, the mother of division ; Episcopacy has in all ages of the Church been looked upon as a bond of Union—the Bishop is the centre of Unity. It is true that there is a much to be regretted separation between the Eastern and Western Church, and again in the Western, between the Roman and Anglican communions ; but yet notwithstanding this separation, the Unity of the Church is still in a sense unbroken, for by the preservation of the Apostolical Succession, all are united in their origin. "As there are many rays of the sun, but one light ; and many branches of a tree, but one strength based in its tenacious root ; and since from one spring flow many streams, although the multiplicity seems diffused in the liberality of an overflowing abundance, yet the Unity is still preserved in the source." But the case is different with those who have cut themselves off from the Apostolical Succession, for, "separate a ray of the sun from its body of light, its Unity does not allow a division of light ; break a branch from a tree—when broken, it will not be able to bud ; cut off the stream from its fountain, and that which is cut off dries up." *

No doubt divisions amongst those who call upon the name of Christ do create a rivalry and act as incentives to zeal ; but are the few advantages of schism, questionable as some of

* Cyprian *On the Unity of the Church*, c. 5.

them are, to outweigh its many evils?—because God turns even the evil into good, are we therefore to do evil that good may come? Christ's words we know were, " not peace but a sword," but no one who has read, however cursorily, that magnificent chapter of S. John (the xvii.), which has been styled the Holy of Holies, or Prayer of the Great High Priest, where occurs the oft-repeated prayer, " Father grant that they may be one, even as we are one,"—no one who has read this chapter can for an instant doubt on which side Christ's mind lay, whether on that of unity or that of division. " God is not the author of confusion but of peace." * He is a God of unity, and it is not to division but to union, to unaminity, that He has promised His blessing. " Jerusalem," we are told, " is built as a city that is at unity in itself." † The Church is " one body." ‡ It is the Lord's body, of which it was said, " not a bone of it shall be broken." ||

Such is the ideal, but alas for the measure of man's sin, which is the difference between God's promise and its fulfilment; how many rents have been made in that robe of the Saviour, which was not to be divided! When we look about and see the many schisms and divisions by which the Church is rent asunder, we feel as if the time could never come on this side the grave when there shall be " one fold under one Shepherd." Yet surely the prayer of the Great High Priest for unity in His Church will not always remain unfulfilled. Thank God, even now the horizon is not all dark : here and there streaks of light shine through the gloom, heralds of the coming day. Small but unmistakeable and ever-increasing tokens there are of a longing in men's hearts after unity. And refreshing it is to find such in these days of scepticism. For with infidelity towering aloft in such a menacing attitude, and knocking at our very gates, an undivided front is especially necessary on the part of those who are on Christ's side, so that the enemy may not have the easy prey of a house divided against itself.

* 1 Cor. xiv. 33.

† Psalm cxxii. 3. (Prayer Book Version.)

‡ Eph. iv. 4.

| S. John xix. 36.

Let us all labour and pray for the peace of Jerusalem. And may He "that maketh men to be of one mind in a house" mercifully grant, "that those who profess and call themselves Christians may be led into the way of truth, and hold the faith in unity of spirit, in the bond of peace, and in righteousness of life."

A. King and Co., Printers and Stereotypers, 2 Upperkirkgate, Aberdeen.